MW00942465

MY FIRST BIBLE REFERENCE

BIBLE MINUTES
for Girls

200 Gotta-Know
People, Places, Ideas & More

BARBOUR **kidz**
A Division of Barbour Publishing

Editorial assistance by Kayla Coons and Jennifer Hahn.

ISBN 978-1-63609-150-1

Published by Barbour Publishing, Inc., 1810 Barbour Drive, Uhrichsville, Ohio 44683, www.barbourbooks.com

Our mission is to inspire the world with the life-changing message of the Bible.

 Member of the
Evangelical Christian
Publishers Association

Printed in the United States of America.

001005 1121 SP

CONTENTS

THERE'S NO MORE IMPORTANT BOOK THAN THE BIBLE.

This book makes learning the Bible fun and easy!

. . . .

This "first Bible reference" was created especially for girls ages 6 and up. Flip through the following pages, and you'll be introduced to some of the Bible's most important names, places, and ideas.

Each of the 200 entries can be easily read and understood in 60 seconds or less. These key bits of knowledge will help you see what God's Word is all about! Plus, if you want to go further, each entry includes a "Learn More" reference that you can look up in your own Bible.

Here's what you'll find inside:

People: 50 important women and men, including Abigail, Deborah, Esther, Eve and Hannah, plus—of course—Jesus, the most important Person ever.

Places: 31 key nations, cities, towns, rivers, lakes, and other spots you should know—in alphabetical order from Antioch through Zarephath.

Events: 49 history-making moments—in order from the Fall of Satan through Heaven Comes to Earth.

Ideas: 42 "theological concepts" (to use a big phrase) that God considered important enough to place in the Bible—from Baptism through Worship.

Names of God: 28 of the most interesting and important names of the Trinity—God the Father, Jesus Christ the Son, and the Holy Spirit.

You'll love the interesting facts and details from scripture, all in a colorful, take-anywhere package. (By the way, when you see a name or word printed in color, that means it has its own entry in the book—be sure to look it up!) *Bible Minutes for Girls* will fire up a lifelong love of learning God's Word!

Abigail

Then David said to Abigail, "Thanks be to the Lord God of Israel, Who sent you this day to meet me."
1 SAMUEL 25:32

Abigail's quick thinking and good advice kept David from making a big mistake. David was running from King Saul, who was trying to kill him. He came across Abigail's land and asked Abigail's husband, Nabal, for food for himself and his army. But Nabal insulted David's men and refused to help them.

David was angry with Nabal, but Abigail ran out to give food to David and his men. She asked him not to hurt her Nabal. Abigail knew it would be a sin for David to kill Nabal and told him that God would want him to make the right choice. David was thankful for Abigail's boldness. After Nabal died, Abigail became David's wife and was the mother to some of his sons.

Learn More: 1 Samuel 25

Abraham

Now the Lord said to Abram, "Leave your country, your family and your father's house, and go to the land that I will show you."
GENESIS 12:1

You may have heard Abraham called "Father Abraham." This nickname is because God promised Abraham that he would be the father of a great nation, with children and grandchildren and great-grandchildren who would be as many as the stars in the sky or grains of sand on the beach. This promise confused Abraham and his wife, though, because God promised this to him when he didn't have *any* children!

It took many years, but God did give Abraham and his wife Sarah a son, Isaac. God would later test Abraham's faith by asking him to sacrifice Isaac. Abraham trusted God and showed his faith by obeying. But God's angel did not let Abraham sacrifice Isaac and provided a ram to be sacrificed instead.

Learn More: Genesis 21:1–8

Adam

Then the Lord God made man from the dust of the ground. And He breathed into his nose the breath of life. Man became a living being.
GENESIS 2:7

Adam was the first human to be created. God had created the earth, the moon, stars, the sun, animals, and all living things by speaking. But on the last day of creation, God took the dust from the ground and breathed His breath into it to create a man, Adam.

God made Adam in charge of the Garden of Eden and all its animals and plants. Adam had the job of naming all of the things he saw in the garden. Can you imagine coming up with new names for animals and plants? It was a big job for just one man. God saw that Adam needed a partner and God created Eve. Together they walked with God in the Garden until they sinned by eating the fruit the serpent gave them.

Learn More: Genesis 2

Anna

At that time she [Anna] came and gave thanks to God. She told the people in Jerusalem about Jesus. They were looking for the One to save them from the punishment of their sins and to set them free.
Luke 2:38

In the time when Jesus lived on earth, firstborn babies were taken to the temple to be dedicated to God. The parents also gave an offering to the Lord. When the Baby was eight days old, His parents—Joseph and Mary, mother of Jesus—took Him to the temple in Jerusalem.

A prophetess named Anna was at the temple that day, fasting and praying. God gave special understanding to Anna so that she knew right away that the infant was Jesus.

Anna praised the Lord because she could see and hold the Messiah. Anna was a very faithful woman. Her husband died when she was young, but she spent the rest of her life serving daily in the temple. She knew the Lord would keep His promise and send the Messiah.

Learn More: Luke 2:36–38

Bathsheba

Bathsheba put her face to the ground in front of the king and said, "May my lord King David live forever."
1 KINGS 1:31

. . . .

Bathsheba and David got married after they sinned against God. God listened to them when they asked for His forgiveness, and He blessed them by giving them a baby boy. Their son, Solomon, was promised to become king when he grew up, after David's days as king were over. But David had older sons who fought because they wanted to become king. They even planned a way to remove David from being king.

Bathsheba found out about the plan against David. She and Nathan, a prophet, told David the sad news so that he could give the throne to Solomon. David crowned Solomon as his heir to the throne instead of the older sons.

. . . .

Learn More: 2 Samuel 11

Daniel

So the king had Daniel brought in and thrown into the place where lions were kept. The king said to Daniel, "May your God, Whom you are faithful to serve, save you."
DANIEL 6:16

When Daniel was young, he was taken away by the Babylonian king, Nebuchadnezzar. Daniel and his friends, Shadrach, Meshach, and Abednego, chose to not eat the king's fancy food or drink his wine. They asked to eat vegetables and drink water instead. Before long, they were healthier and stronger than the other boys in the palace. This pleased King Nebuchadnezzar.

Daniel continued to show his faith through the years. Some evil men in the new king's court told the king to make a law saying nobody could worship God or pray to Him. But Daniel kept praying to God, even when it was against the law. He was punished by being thrown into a den of lions. Because of his faith and God's protection, Daniel was not harmed. This miracle caused King Darius to worship God and declare His power in front of the nation.

Learn More: Daniel 6

David

Then David said to the Philistine, "You come to me with a sword and spears. But I come to you in the name of the Lord of All, the God of the armies of Israel, Whom you have stood against."
1 SAMUEL 17:45

David was just a boy when he became a great warrior. He was visiting his brothers who were fighting against an army of Philistines when he heard a giant, Goliath, insulting the Lord God. The army of Israel was afraid to fight the giant, but not David. David knew he had God's power with him. He gathered five smooth stones and his sling and met Goliath on the battlefield. David flung the stone and it killed Goliath.

David became famous among the people for his wisdom and great skill as a warrior. King Saul became jealous of him and wanted to kill him, but God protected David. David would be the king God chose to lead His people! Even though he made some bad choices in life, David would always ask the Lord to forgive him. That's why he is called "a man after God's own heart."

Learn More: 1 Samuel 17

Deborah

*And the people of Israel came to her [Deborah]
to find out what was right or wrong.*
JUDGES 4:5

Deborah was an amazing woman of God. She was a prophetess who warned Israel when they were making bad decisions that went against God's law. She was also a judge who told the people if what they were doing was right or wrong. She used wisdom to help solve disagreements between people.

When Israel was going into a battle, she told a military leader, Barak, what to do to win against the Canaanite army. But Barak told Deborah that he would not go into battle unless she went with him. He believed Deborah knew what God wanted, so Barak wanted her on the battlefield. Deborah and Barak led the Israelites into battle and the Lord let them win. When the battle was over, the two leaders sang a song of praise to the Lord.

Learn More: Judges 4:1–16

Dorcas

A woman who was a follower lived in the city of Joppa. Her name was Tabitha, or Dorcas. She did many good things and many acts of kindness.
ACTS 9:36

A woman named Dorcas, or Tabitha in the Aramaic language, was a woman known for her good deeds to help the people of Joppa. She made clothes and helped the widows in her town. When she became sick and died, the people were very sad. They begged the apostle Peter to come to her house.

Peter went, and he told the crowds to leave the room where her body was lying. Peter told Dorcas to get up, and she opened her eyes and was alive again!

Peter called the people back into the room so that they could see that Dorcas was alive and well. Many people in Joppa heard about Jesus and became His followers because of this miracle.

Learn More: Acts 9:36–42

Elijah

Then the woman said to Elijah, "Now I know that you are a man of God. Now I know that the word of the Lord in your mouth is truth."
1 KINGS 17:24

King Ahab was an evil king who worshipped a false god and did things that were wrong in God's sight. Elijah was a prophet of the one true God. He challenged the fake prophets of the fake god Baal to a contest. Elijah said that if God brought down fire upon the altar he built, then He was the true God. But if Baal brought down fire to the altar the prophets built, then he was the true god. The prophets of Baal cried out to their false god all day and nothing happened. When evening came, Elijah asked God to bring down fire to prove that He was the one true God. You know what? God's fire fell on the altar, burning up the sacrifice and everything around it! This proved to everyone that God alone was worthy of worship.

Learn More: 1 Kings 18:20–40

Elizabeth

*When Elizabeth heard Mary speak, the baby
moved in her body. At the same time
Elizabeth was filled with the Holy Spirit.*
LUKE 1:41

Elizabeth was an old woman when an angel appeared to her husband, Zacharias. The angel said that Zacharias and Elizabeth would have a baby who they should name John. The angel also said that John would be a prophet just like Elijah was, telling people about the coming Messiah.

Elizabeth had been pregnant for six months with their miracle son when her cousin Mary, mother of Jesus, came to visit. Mary was pregnant with Jesus, and when she spoke, John jumped inside Elizabeth's belly! Elizabeth praised God for the amazing things that were happening. Elizabeth's son would grow up to be John the Baptist, the man who told others about the coming of Jesus Christ.

Learn More: Luke 1:26–44

Esther

Queen Esther answered, "If I have found favor in your eyes, O king, and if it please the king, I ask that my life and the lives of my people be saved."
ESTHER 7:3

. . . .

Esther was an orphaned girl who was raised by her cousin, Mordecai. She was a Jew in the land of Persia, ruled by King Ahasuerus. When the king was looking for a new queen, he chose Esther for her beauty and grace. She did not want anyone to find out she was Jewish, because Mordecai told her it might bring her harm.

Several years later, the king's official, Haman, came up with a plot to kill the Jews living in Persia. Then he convinced the king to make it a law. Mordecai found out and told his cousin Esther that she could do something to save her people.

Queen Esther made a bold move that was against the law—she went to the king without being invited. Esther risked her life to save the lives of others. Her courage and bravery spared the Jews in Persia.

. . . .

Learn More: Esther 4

Eve

The Lord God made woman from the bone which He had taken from the man. And He brought her to the man.
GENESIS 2:22

God created Adam as the first man on earth. When God saw that Adam was lonely, the Lord made him fall into a deep sleep. While Adam rested, God took one of the man's ribs and created a woman from it. She would be called Eve, which means "the mother of all living."

God gave Adam and Eve just one rule: they were not to eat from one tree in the garden, the Tree of Knowledge of Good and Evil. God's enemy, Satan, showed up looking like a snake. He told Eve that if she ate of the tree, she would be like God. Eve thought that sounded good, so she ate the fruit. Then she shared some with Adam. But that was a sin against God and it messed up every human being for all time. Eve's story shows us that even those who walk close to God can be tempted to sin. We must ask God's Holy Spirit to help us overcome temptation.

Learn More: Genesis 2–3.

Hannah

"So I [Hannah] have given him [Samuel] to the Lord. He is given to the Lord as long as he lives."
And they worshiped the Lord there.
1 SAMUEL 1:28

Hannah was sad because she had not been able to have children. She went to the worship center and prayed, telling God about her problem and how sad it made her. Hannah promised God that if He would bless her with a son, she would let him serve God with the priests. The Lord answered her prayer, and Hannah did have a son. She named him Samuel, which means "heard of God," because she had asked God for a son and He heard her prayer.

When Samuel was about two years old, Hannah kept her promise by giving the little boy to the high priest, Eli. Samuel learned from Eli and helped in the tabernacle. When he was grown, Samuel became a great priest and prophet who anointed Saul and David as the first two kings of Israel.

Learn More: 1 Samuel 1:9–28

Huldah

*So Hilkiah, the religious leader, Ahikam,
Achbor, Shaphan and Asaiah went to
Huldah the woman who spoke for God.*
2 Kings 22:14

Hilkiah, the high priest, was getting ready for the temple to be repaired. He found a copy of the book of the law. Some of the religious leaders read parts of it to King Josiah. The king was upset because he realized the people of Judah had turned away from the law. They had begun to worship false gods! So Josiah sent the leaders to ask Huldah the prophetess if God would judge them because of these sins.

The prophetess had bad news and good news for Josiah. Yes, she told him, the Lord's judgment would come to the nation, but it wouldn't happen until after Josiah had passed away.

Her prophecy was fulfilled about 30 years later when the army of Babylon captured Jerusalem. Huldah is one of the few female prophets mentioned in the Bible.

Learn More: 2 Chronicles 34:22–28

Isaac

But God said, "No, but your wife Sarah will give birth to your son. And you will give him the name Isaac. I will make My agreement with him and for his children after him, an agreement that will last forever."
GENESIS 17:19

God promised Abraham that his descendants—his children and their children and their children over many, many years—would become a great nation. The promise began to be fulfilled when Isaac was born to Abraham and Sarah in their old age.

When Isaac was young, the Lord tested Abraham's faith by asking him to offer Isaac as a sacrifice. But just as Abraham raised a knife to take the boy's life, God stopped him and sent a ram for an offering instead.

The Bible describes Isaac as a person who trusted God and lived a quiet life of simple faith (Hebrews 11:17–20).

Isaac was the father of twin sons, Jacob and Esau. Jacob's sons were the leaders of the twelve tribes that became the nation of Israel.

Learn More: Genesis 21:1–8

Isaiah

This is what Isaiah the son of Amoz saw about Judah and Jerusalem that was coming.

ISAIAH 2:1

. . . .

Isaiah was chosen to be a prophet to Israel and Judah when God gave the man a vision of Himself. Isaiah saw the Lord seated on His heavenly throne, surrounded by angels and smoke. God asked whom He should send to speak to the people. Isaiah responded, "Here am I. Send me!" (Isaiah 6:8).

Isaiah spoke God's message to several kings of Judah in the capital city of Jerusalem. He warned that the nation would be destroyed by Assyria unless the people stopped worshipping false gods and turned back to the Lord (Isaiah 10:1–10). Isaiah spoke more about the coming Messiah—Jesus—than any other Old Testament prophet.

. . . .

Learn More: 2 Kings 20

Jacob

*So Jacob gave the place the name of Peniel. For he said,
"I have seen God face to face, and yet I am still alive."*
GENESIS 32:30

Jacob tricked both his brother and his father into giving him valuable gifts that were not meant for him. Afraid of what his brother, Esau, might do to him, Jacob ran away. One night, he had a dream that angels were going up and down a stairway into heaven. At the top stood God Himself. He promised Jacob that He would fulfill His covenant—His important promise—to him and his descendants.

Later, Jacob had another strange experience— a wrestling match with the Lord. The battle left Jacob with a limp, but God blessed him and gave him the new name *Israel*, meaning "he wrestles with God." Now Jacob was ready to fulfill the purpose God had for his life. Jacob would have twelve sons whose descendants became the twelve tribes of Israel.

Learn More: Genesis 32:22–32

Jael

Jael went out to meet Sisera, saying, "Come in, my lord. Come in to me. Do not be afraid." So he went into her tent, and she put a cover over him.
JUDGES 4:18

Deborah was a prophetess and judge of Israel. It was unusual for a woman to serve as judge. And God told here that another woman would kill the commander of an enemy army. Sisera, Canaan's commander, ran away after his army lost to Israel. He came to the tent of a woman named Jael, hoping for safety. Jael was kind to Sisera and gave him milk to drink. She said that she would hide Sisera in her tent. Jael even promised him that if he fell asleep and any enemies came close, she would warn him. But when he fell asleep, Jael killed Sisera.

Deborah celebrated Israel's victory and sang a song to the Lord. She honored Jael, calling her "the most respected of women" for defeating the leader of Canaan.

Learn More: Judges 4:17–22

Jesus

Long ago God spoke to our early fathers in many different ways. He spoke through the early preachers. But in these last days He has spoken to us through His Son. God gave His Son everything. It was by His Son that God made the world.

HEBREWS 1:1–2

Jesus was born in a stable in Bethlehem while Herod the Great was king. Jesus was born to a young woman named Mary. God's Holy Spirit caused her to get pregnant. Jesus grew up like a regular boy, but He knew what God the Father had sent Him to do on earth. When He became a man, Jesus preached and healed, taught about the kingdom of God, and went looking for those who did not know about God.

Jesus had a ministry on earth that lasted three years—from the time He was baptized by John the Baptist until He was betrayed by Judas and captured by the Jewish leaders. Jesus was accused of doing wrong, even though He had not done anything wrong at all. Jesus was put to death on a cross. Then He was buried in a tomb, but on the third day, He rose from the dead! Forty days later, Jesus went back to heaven where He is waiting for the time that He will return again for all those who follow Him.

Learn More: Colossians 1:12–29

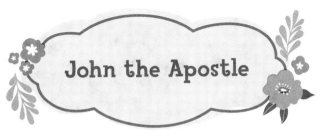

John the Apostle

*Going from there, Jesus saw two other brothers.
They were James and John, the sons of Zebedee.
They were sitting in a boat with their father,
mending their nets. Jesus called them.*

MATTHEW 4:21

John was one of the first disciples chosen by Jesus. He and his brother James were working on their fishing nets on the Sea of Galilee when Jesus invited them to follow Him and become "fishers of men."

We read about John many times throughout the Gospels, and he called himself "the disciple Jesus loved" in John, the Gospel he wrote.

While He was on the cross, Jesus asked John to take care of His mother. The Lord knew He would be returning to heaven, so He made sure Mary, mother of Jesus, was cared for. After Jesus left, John worked with the apostle Peter in Jerusalem to tell people about the Gospel. Later, he wrote several books of the New Testament—including the three letters of John and the book of Revelation.

Learn More: Mark 5:37–42

John the Baptist

John the Baptist preached in the desert.
He preached that people should be baptized
because they were sorry for their sins and had
turned from them. And they would be forgiven.
MARK 1:4

When people heard John the Baptist speak, they thought he was a lot like the prophet Elijah from many years before. John lived in the wilderness and told people to stop their sinning. He told them to get baptized to show they were serious about following God. Jesus even began His ministry by asking to be baptized by John.

John the Baptist was later put into prison by King Herod Antipas. John sent his followers to ask Jesus if He was the Messiah, the One that Israel had been waiting for. Jesus reminded John of His preaching and healing in the name of God the Father—that proved Jesus was who He claimed to be. Then Jesus said something very nice: "Of those born of women, there is no one greater than John the Baptist" (Matthew 11:11).

Learn More: Mark 1:1–8

Jonah

The Lord sent a big fish to swallow Jonah, and he was in the stomach of the fish for three days and three nights.
JONAH 1:17

God told Jonah to preach to the people of Assyria, an enemy nation that Israel hated. But Jonah did not want to obey God's command. So he got on board a ship that would take him in the opposite direction.

As punishment for his disobedience, the Lord sent a huge fish to swallow Jonah. Jonah was in the belly of the fish for three days and nights. God then had the fish spit him up on dry land. This time, Jonah went directly to Assyria's capital city.

When Jonah preached the message God gave him, the people asked forgiveness for their sins and turned to the Lord. That's good news! But Jonah was disappointed that they would not be punished. Jonah was reminded that God's love isn't just for certain people—it is for all people and nations of the world.

Learn More: Jonah 4

Joseph, Son of Jacob

*"So it was not you who sent me here, but God.
He has made me a father to Pharaoh, and ruler
of all his house, and of all the land of Egypt."*
GENESIS 45:8

Joseph was born to Jacob's favorite wife, Rachel. His brothers knew Joseph was their father's favorite and they were jealous of him. They came up with a plan to kill him. His brother, Judah, told them not to kill him but to sell him as a slave instead. After they sold him, they lied to their father, saying Joseph was dead, to cover up what they had done.

In Egypt, Joseph became known for his ability to interpret dreams, including one for Pharaoh, the king. Because of his ability to explain Pharaoh's dream, Joseph was made second-in-command of all Egypt.

Joseph's brothers came to Egypt to buy grain during a famine in their land, and Joseph forgave them for the wrong they did to him. Joseph invited his family to Egypt to escape the famine, saving them from death.

Learn More: Genesis 37

Joshua

"No man will be able to stand against you [Joshua] all the days of your life. I will be with you just as I have been with Moses. I will be faithful to you and will not leave you alone."
JOSHUA 1:5

Joshua was one of the Israelites who were led out of Egypt by Moses. He was even one of the twelve spies sent into the Promised Land. Only two of the spies, Joshua and Caleb, were confident that they could take the land by God's power.

Joshua became the leader of the Israelites after Moses' death. God told Joshua many times not to be afraid because He would be with him.

The first city that Joshua battled was Jericho. Its thick walls fell after the Israelites marched around the city silently for six days and then blew trumpets and shouted on the seventh day. God was showing His people that they could only enter the Promised Land by His power.

Learn More: Joshua 6

Lazarus

When He [Jesus] had said this, He called with a loud voice, "Lazarus, come out!"
JOHN 11:43

Jesus was teaching near Jerusalem when He learned that His friend Lazarus was very sick. Jesus waited two days before going to Bethany, where Lazarus lived with his sisters, Mary and Martha. Jesus often stayed in their home when preaching and healing in and around Jerusalem. When Jesus arrived, Martha met Him with the news that Lazarus had died.

Jesus promised Martha that her brother would live again because He had the power to bring dead people back to life. Then He called Lazarus out of the tomb with three simple words: "Lazarus, come out!" Lazarus came out of the tomb still wearing his burial clothes. This miracle caused many to believe that Jesus was the Son of God.

Learn More: John 11

Leah

When the morning came, Jacob saw that it was Leah. He said to Laban, "What have you done to me? Did I not work for you for Rachel? Why have you fooled me?"
GENESIS 29:25

Imagine how surprised Jacob must have been. He thought he was marrying Rachel, but he ended up being married to her sister, Leah, instead!

Jacob got a job working for Laban, Leah and Rachel's father. Laban promised Jacob he could marry Rachel if he would work for him for seven years. But on the day of the wedding, Laban had his older daughter, Leah, dress up as the bride. Jacob didn't realize he had been tricked until the next morning. So the sneaky Laban told Jacob that if he worked for seven more years, he could marry Rachel, the one who Jacob loved and had wanted to marry.

Jacob always loved Rachel more than Leah and didn't treat Leah as kindly. But Leah became the mother of six of his twelve sons, and years later, their relatives would be men who led six of the twelve tribes of Israel.

Learn More: Genesis 29:15–30

Lois

*I remember your true faith. It is the same faith your
grandmother Lois had and your mother Eunice had.
I am sure you have that same faith also.*

2 TIMOTHY 1:5

. . . .

Lois was the grandmother of Timothy, who was a missionary student of the apostle Paul. While he was growing up, she helped her grandson learn about the Lord. Paul spoke well of Lois and praised her for teaching her grandson how to live the way Jesus would want him to live.

Paul also said the same thing about Timothy's mother, Eunice. Maybe Lois had taught her daughter about the Lord, and then Eunice taught her son how to live as a Christian should.

Lois was a good guide for Timothy, and today, many parents and grandparents still can be good teachers to their kids and grandkids about how to be a follower of Jesus.

Lydia

One of the women who listened sold purple cloth. She was from the city of Thyatira. Her name was Lydia and she was a worshiper of God. The Lord opened her heart to hear what Paul said.

ACTS 16:14

. . . .

The apostle Paul stopped at the city of Philippi with Timothy and Silas while he was on his second missionary journey. On the Sabbath, they went to a river that was close by, looking for people who wanted to hear about Jesus. When they got there, they found a group of women who had gathered to pray. Among them was a woman named Lydia, who sold cloth colored with a purple dye. She listened carefully to Paul when he spoke about the Gospel. She believed what she heard and decided to follow Jesus and was baptized. Other family members also chose to believe in Jesus.

Lydia was probably the first person to become a Christian in Philippi. She invited Paul and his missionary friends to stay at her house while they preached and served in the city.

. . . .

Learn More: Acts 16:11–15

Martha

Jesus said to her, "Martha, Martha, you are worried and troubled about many things."
LUKE 10:41

From Martha, we can learn a valuable lesson about what is really important in life. Jesus was a guest in her home in Bethany, where she lived with her sister Mary and their brother Lazarus. Martha was busy in the kitchen, probably fixing a meal for Jesus. But Mary was sitting at Jesus' feet, listening to Him as He taught.

Martha was frustrated with Mary because she was not helping with the meal. She asked Jesus to tell Mary to help her in preparing the food. Jesus replied that Martha was busy with things that did not matter in the long run, while Mary, sister of Martha, had chosen to do what was most important at the time—spending time with Him.

Learn More: Luke 10:39–42

Mary, Mother of Jesus

The angel said to her, "Mary, do not be afraid. You have found favor with God."
LUKE 1:30

Mary was a teenage girl from the village of Nazareth who was engaged to be married to a carpenter named Joseph. She was shocked when the angel Gabriel told her she would give birth to Jesus, the Son of God. She could hardly believe this since she was not married. How could she have a baby?

The angel told her that it would be a miracle and that God Himself would give her the baby. Mary understood how blessed she was to have been chosen to have this promised baby. She raised Jesus with her husband, Joseph.

Mary would later see Jesus' first miracle at a wedding at Cana as well as His death on the cross.

Learn More: Luke 1:26–38

Mary, Sister of Martha

Mary took a jar of special perfume that cost much money and poured it on the feet of Jesus. She dried His feet with her hair. The house was filled with the smell of the special perfume.
JOHN 12:3

Mary lived with her sister Martha and their brother Lazarus in the village of Bethany. During one of Jesus' visits to their home, He praised Mary for sitting at His feet and listening to His teachings. When her brother Lazarus died, Mary was sad in her own quiet way and stayed inside the house while her sister went out to meet Jesus. When Martha called Mary to come outside, she knelt at Jesus' feet, weeping.

After Jesus brought Lazarus back to life, Mary showed her thankfulness by pouring expensive perfume on His feet and wiping them with her hair. One of the disciples complained about how she was wasting the expensive perfume, but Jesus used it to teach about the time when He would die. Jesus said, "Let her alone. She has kept it for the time when I will be buried" (John 12:7).

Learn More: John 12:1–8

Mary Magdalene

*Mary Magdalene went and told the followers
that she had seen the Lord. She told
them the things He had said to her.*
JOHN 20:18

Mary was from the village of Magdala, so she was known as Mary Magdalene. Jesus had healed her when she was possessed by demons, and she became one of His most loyal followers. Mary, along with other women, made meals for Him and His disciples.

Mary was one of the women who were at the cross when Jesus was crucified. She came to His tomb on resurrection morning to finish preparing His body for burial by anointing Him with oils. But when she got there, she found that the tomb was empty (Mark 16:1–8)!

The Gospel of John tells that Jesus appeared to Mary first after He rose from the dead. He gave her the instruction to go report to the disciples that she had seen Him alive. To prove that what Mary told them was true, Jesus appeared to them later that same day.

Learn More: John 20:11–20

Miriam

Miriam said to them, "Sing to the Lord, for He is praised for His greatness. He has thrown the horse and horseman into the sea."
EXODUS 15:21

It is thought that Miriam is the sister of Moses who is described in Exodus 2. Moses' caring sister watched over him after he had been laid in a basket in the grass beside the Nile River. She spoke to Pharaoh's daughter after she had found him and offered to find a Hebrew mother who would care for him.

Later, when Moses had guided the Hebrews through the Red Sea, Miriam led the women in dancing, singing, and playing instruments, thanking the Lord for protecting His people. There was a time that Miriam showed disrespect to Moses by questioning his leadership, and God gave her a skin disease. But Moses prayed for her, and she was healed of the leprosy.

Learn More: Exodus 2:1–8

Moses

*Then the Lord said to Moses, "Go to Pharaoh
and say to him, 'The Lord says this: "Let My
people go, so they may worship Me.'"*
Exodus 8:1

God spoke face to face with Moses "as a man speaks to
his friend" (Exodus 33:11). With the help of his brother,
Aaron, Moses led the Israelites out of slavery in Egypt
and brought them to the border of the Promised Land.

At first, Moses made excuses to try to avoid obeying
God. God let Moses know that He would be with Moses
all along the way. Believing God's promise, Moses brought
ten plagues against Egypt. These terrible plagues—things
like the river turning to blood and the death of all of
Egypt's firstborn children—finally caused Pharaoh to
let the Israelites go.

Moses then led the people through the wilderness
for more than 40 years. Along the way, God told Moses
how to get food and water, gave him the Ten Commandments (special instructions for the people's behavior),
and helped him build the tabernacle, a place for the
people to worship.

Learn More: Hebrews 11:23–26

Noah

And Noah did all that the Lord told him to do.
GENESIS 7:5

Noah was a man who followed God—even in a time when the whole world had become evil. The Lord told Noah that He planned to destroy all living things with a great flood. But Noah and his family would be safe if he would build a giant boat, also called "the ark." Noah obeyed the Lord, built the ark, and entered it with his family and two of every kind of animal. Then it began to rain. The rain lasted 40 days, and water covered the whole earth.

After the flood was over, Noah built an altar and offered a sacrifice of thanksgiving to God. The Lord told Noah that He would never again flood the whole world. He sealed His promise with a rainbow in the sky.

Learn More: Genesis 8

Paul

He fell to the ground. Then he heard a voice say,
"Saul, Saul, why are you working so hard against Me?"
Acts 9:4

Paul, who was called Saul when he was born, was a Jewish religious leader who punished and sometimes killed Christians shortly after Jesus went back to heaven. When Paul was on a trip to Damascus to hurt more Christians, he had an unexpected meeting with God. This meeting changed Saul's life, as well as his name!

Soon, Paul was a powerful Christian and one of the first missionaries for the Gospel. During his ministry, Paul wrote 13 letters that are part of our Bible today. They were meant to encourage the churches he founded as well as the people who served with him in his missionary work. These letters—Romans, 1 and 2 Corinthians, Galatians, Ephesians, Philippians, Colossians, 1 and 2 Thessalonians, 1 and 2 Timothy, Titus, and Philemon—make up about one-fourth of the New Testament!

Learn More: Acts 9:1–31

Peter

Simon Peter said, "You are the Christ,
the Son of the living God."
MATTHEW 16:16

Peter and his brother, Andrew, were two of the twelve disciples who stayed with Jesus through His three-year ministry. Peter was the first disciple to recognize Jesus as the Messiah—God's chosen One—and understand the reason He came to earth.

Peter promised he would always be faithful to Jesus. But then on the night Jesus was arrested, Peter said three times that he didn't even *know* Him! Jesus forgave Peter, and he became bold in telling others about Jesus. On the day of Pentecost, when God sent His Spirit to live in believers, Peter preached a famous sermon that caused 3,000 people to follow Jesus (Acts 2:14–41). In his later years, Peter wrote the New Testament books of 1 and 2 Peter.

Learn More: Matthew 14:24–33

Priscilla

Greet Priscilla and Aquila. They worked with me for Christ. They almost died for me. I am thankful for them. All the churches that were started among the people who are not Jews are thankful for them also.
ROMANS 16:3–4

Priscilla was a follower of Jesus who, along with her husband, Aquila, almost died for the apostle Paul. They were great helpers in several of the churches he began. We don't know how they risked their lives for Paul, but it's clear that Priscilla and Aquila helped him in his work with the Ephesian believers. After Paul left Ephesus, Priscilla and her husband stayed behind and taught a powerful speaker named Apollos more about Christianity.

The couple, with Paul, sent greetings to the Christ followers at Corinth. He wrote this letter from Ephesus and mentioned that a house church was meeting at that time in Priscilla and Aquila's home (1 Corinthians 16:19).

Learn More: Acts 18:18–28

Rachel

Jacob loved Rachel. So he said, "I will serve you seven years for your younger daughter Rachel."
GENESIS 29:18

Rachel first caught Jacob's eye when he arrived in Haran while running away from his brother, Esau. Jacob stayed with his uncle, Laban, and worked out an agreement to marry Laban's daughter, Rachel. He promised to work seven years before marrying her. But on the wedding day, Laban tricked Jacob into marrying her older sister, Leah, instead. Then Jacob had to work seven more years to have Rachel as his wife.

Rachel was Jacob's favorite wife, but she was not able to have children. She was jealous of her sister, who had several sons with Jacob. After many years of being unable to have children, Rachel did eventually have two sons—Benjamin and Joseph, son of Jacob.

Learn More: Genesis 30:22–26

Rahab

And she [Rahab] said to the men, "I know that the Lord has given you the land. The fear of you has come upon us. All the people living in the land have become weak with fear because of you."
JOSHUA 2:9

Soon after the Israelites entered the Promised Land, Joshua sent spies to figure out how strong Jericho was. It was a mighty city in Canaan. The spies went to the home of a woman named Rahab so that they could avoid attention that might get them in trouble. But people found out that they were there, and soldiers were sent to arrest them.

The spies asked Rahab to let them hide on the roof of her house. When she agreed to it, they promised to spare her and her family when Joshua and his warriors destroyed the city. She helped them escape to safety by letting them down over the city wall through a window in her house.

After Israel conquered Jericho, Rahab and her family became Israelites. Through her line of relatives, King David was born, and after more generations, the Messiah came. She is one of only five women listed in Matthew's list of Jesus' ancestors.

Learn More: Joshua 2

Rebekah

Then Isaac brought Rebekah into his mother Sarah's tent, and she became his wife. And he loved her. So Isaac found comfort after his mother's death.
GENESIS 24:67

Isaac's father, Abraham, sent his servant back to his ancestors' country of Haran for an important job. The servant was to find a wife for Isaac after his mother, Sarah, died. Isaac was very pleased when the servant brought Rebekah to him.

Rebekah and Isaac had twin sons, Esau and Jacob. Jacob was Rebekah's favorite because he stayed near home with her in the tents while Esau went out to hunt for food. Along with Jacob, Rebekah came up with a plan to trick Isaac into blessing Jacob rather than his older brother, Esau. When Esau threatened to kill Jacob, Rebekah sent him to live with her brother Laban for protection.

Learn More: Genesis 27

Ruth

But Ruth said, "Do not beg me to leave you or turn away from following you. I will go where you go. I will live where you live. Your people will be my people. And your God will be my God."
RUTH 1:16

. . . .

Because of a famine in Bethlehem, a Jewish family—Naomi, her husband, and her two sons—moved to the country of Moab. Her sons married women from there. But while they were in Moab, Naomi's husband and sons died. Naomi and the two younger women were left without any male relatives to help them.

One of Naomi's daughters-in-law was Ruth. When Naomi decided to return to Bethlehem, Ruth wanted to go with her, even though that meant leaving her own relatives behind.

In Bethlehem, because they needed food, Ruth went to the fields to gather grain left behind by harvesters. She met the landowner, Boaz, who was a distant relative of Naomi.

Naomi encouraged Ruth to become friends with Boaz. Soon, Boaz and Ruth married, and Ruth gave birth to a son named Obed, who would be the grandfather of King David.

. . . .

Learn More: Ruth 1–4

Samson

Then the woman gave birth to a son and named him Samson. The child grew up and the Lord brought good to him.
JUDGES 13:24

Samson was promised for service to the Lord even before he was born. An angel told his mother that he was to be a Nazirite—a person who would not drink strong drinks or cut his hair. As he grew up, he was set apart for the Lord to use to help His people.

Samson was the last of the judges (or "deliverers") of Israel and was a great warrior against the Philistines. God gave him incredible strength to defeat their armies. But Samson let himself be tricked by a Philistine woman who found out the secret to his strength—his promise to God. She had someone cut his hair while he slept, and he became weak. The Philistines captured Samson and laughed at him. But God allowed him one final moment of strength. Samson knocked down a Philistine temple, killing himself and many of his enemies.

Learn More: Judges 16:28–31

Samuel

Then the Lord came and stood and called as He did
the other times, "Samuel! Samuel!" And Samuel
said, "Speak, for Your servant is listening."
1 SAMUEL 3:10

The prophet Samuel was born in answer to the prayer of his mother, Hannah, who had not been able to have children. To show her thanks to the Lord, she promised that she would give Samuel back to God's service. Hannah took little Samuel to live with Eli, the high priest of Israel.

Samuel obeyed the Lord, and he was faithful to tell God's message to others. God told Samuel to anoint— pour oil over the head of—Saul, showing him to be the Lord's choice as the first king of Israel. When Saul disobeyed the Lord, Samuel anointed a new king from the sons of Jesse. God made it clear to Samuel that David, the youngest son of the family, was His choice as Saul's replacement.

Samuel appears in the New Testament's list of heroes of the faith (Hebrews 11:32).

Learn More: 1 Samuel 3

Sarah

But God said, "No, but your wife Sarah will give birth to your son. And you will give him the name Isaac. I will make My agreement with him and for his children after him, an agreement that will last forever."
GENESIS 17:19

Abraham's wife, Sarah, was not able to have children. That's why Abraham and Sarah were confused when God promised that they would have grandchildren and great-grandchildren and a future family that were as many as the stars in the sky. Sarah doubted God's promise. . .but when God says He'll do something, He will.

When Sarah was 90, she and Abraham finally had their promised son. They called him Isaac, a name meaning "laughter," because Sarah had laughed when the Lord told her she would have a son in her old age (Genesis 18:11–15).

Learn More: Genesis 17:15–21

Solomon

*"So give Your servant [Solomon] an
understanding heart to judge Your people
and know the difference between good and bad.
For who is able to judge Your many people?"*
1 KINGS 3:9

Solomon was the son of King David and Bathsheba. He wasn't David's oldest son, so he should not have been the one to be crowned the next king. But God had chosen Solomon to reign after David. Solomon asked the Lord not for money or power or fame, but for wisdom to rule the people well.

Solomon's leadership and trade deals made both his kingdom and himself rich. He wrote down many wise sayings in the book of Proverbs. Sadly, Solomon foolishly married many women—around 700 of them! They turned his heart away from God. Some people think Solomon wrote the book of Ecclesiastes late in life, when he had returned to obeying God.

Learn More: 1 Kings 3

Stephen

*He was filled with the Holy Spirit. As he looked up
to heaven, he saw the shining-greatness of God
and Jesus standing at the right side of God.*
ACTS 7:55

Stephen was a follower of Jesus in the early church in Jerusalem. There were people who believed in Jesus who did not have enough to eat, and it was Stephen's job to make sure they received the food they needed (Acts 6:1–7).

Stephen accused the Jewish religious leaders of being the ones who killed Jesus the Messiah. He said they were just like their ancestors, who had murdered God's prophets in Old Testament times. When he said that he had seen a vision of God in heaven, with Jesus at His side, the Jewish leaders became so angry that they killed him.

The punishment of Christians increased, so many who believed in Jesus left Jerusalem for safety. As they went to different areas, they took the Gospel to parts of the world where people had not yet heard the Good News.

Learn More: Acts 6:8–60

Thomas

Jesus said to him, "Thomas, because you have seen Me, you believe. Those are happy who have never seen Me and yet believe!"
JOHN 20:29

All twelve of Jesus' disciples had a hard time believing He had been raised from the dead. But Thomas was the biggest doubter of all.

Thomas was not with the rest of the group when Jesus appeared to them on the day of His resurrection. The others told Thomas they had seen Him alive, but he was not convinced. He told the others that he would not believe that Jesus was alive unless he could see the nail marks in His hands.

Eight days later, Jesus appeared again to His disciples. He invited Thomas to touch His wounds. This time Thomas believed and gladly said that Jesus was his Lord and Master.

Learn More: John 20:24–31

Zaccheus

He [Zaccheus] ran ahead and got up into a sycamore tree to see Him. Jesus was going by that way.
LUKE 19:4

Zaccheus was a Jewish man who worked for the Roman government as a tax collector. He cheated other Jews and kept the money for himself. One day as Jesus passed through Jericho on His way to Jerusalem, Zaccheus wanted to get a look at Him. Since Zaccheus was not tall enough, he climbed a tree to get a better view. The tax collector must have been shocked when Jesus called to him by name. Then Jesus invited Himself to Zaccheus's house for a visit!

As he talked with Jesus, Zaccheus realized that he needed to repent for the things he had done wrong. He wanted to make things right again, so he promised to pay people back four times as much as he had taken from them!

Learn More: Luke 19:1–10

Antioch

When [Barnabas] found Saul, he brought him back with him to Antioch. For a year they taught many people in the church. The followers were first called Christians in Antioch.
ACTS 11:26

Antioch was a city about 300 miles north of Jerusalem. It was one of the largest cities in the Roman Empire during New Testament times. After Stephen was put to death in Jerusalem for sharing his belief that Jesus was the Messiah, many believers left for Antioch.

The church in Antioch became larger, with both Jews and Gentiles. It was led by Barnabas and Paul, and it is where the name "Christian" was first used to describe those who followed Jesus.

Learn More: Acts 11:19–26

Ararat, Mount

And in the seventh month, on the seventeenth day of the month, the large boat came to rest on Mount Ararat.

GENESIS 8:4

. . . .

After the Great Flood that destroyed the whole world, Noah's ark came to rest on a mountain. There is a mountain range and a specific mountain peak called Ararat.

Today, we do not know for sure where Noah's ark landed. Some believe it was where the countries of Armenia, Turkey, and Iran all come together. The Tigris and Euphrates rivers have their start in this area. Some searches have tried to locate Noah's ark, but it has not been found yet.

Asia

This is John writing to the seven churches in the country of Asia. May you have loving-favor and peace from God Who was and Who is and Who is to come. May you have loving-favor and peace from the seven Spirits who are before His throne.
REVELATION 1:4

PLACES

John the apostle, Peter, and Paul all wrote to the churches in Asia. But this was not Asia as we think of it today, as the continent containing China and India. "Asia" was a Roman province north of Greece. In Acts, we read that Paul spent two years in Ephesus, the capital city of Asia, teaching in a Jewish place of worship. Because of Paul's work there, we see that "all the Jews and the Greeks in the countries of Asia heard the Word of the Lord" (Acts 19:10). All of the Jews and Greeks heard about Jesus because of Paul's missionary journey there!

Learn More: Acts 19:8–10

Athens

While Paul was waiting for Silas and Timothy in Athens, his spirit was troubled as he saw the whole city worshiping false gods.
ACTS 17:16

The apostle Paul visited Athens during his second missionary journey. Athens was the center of Greek culture for about 500 years before Paul arrived. While Paul was waiting for Timothy and Silas to join him in Athens, he saw many shrines to false gods that could be found all over the city.

After Paul preached in the Jewish place of worship, a group of Greek philosophers wanted to hear more about the "strange" things he was teaching. Most of these philosophers made fun of Paul for his claim that God had raised Jesus from the dead. But a few were eager to hear more, and at least two chose to become Christians.

Learn More: Acts 17:15–34

Babylon

At that time the servants of Nebuchadnezzar
king of Babylon went up to Jerusalem.
His soldiers gathered around the city.
2 KINGS 24:10

The prophet Jeremiah warned God's people that Babylon would take them as captives if they did not stop worshipping false gods. In 587 BC (that means about 587 years before Jesus was born), the Babylonians did capture Judah and took the people as prisoners.

The Babylonians became very powerful when King Nebuchadnezzar ruled. They defeated many nations around them. Ezra 5:14 says, "Nebuchadnezzar had taken the gold and silver objects of the house of God from the house in Jerusalem, and brought them to the house of worship at Babylon." About 50 years later, God allowed the Persian empire to take over Babylon.

Learn More: Ezra 5:12–17

Bethany

Jesus led them out as far as Bethany. Then He lifted up His hands and prayed that good would come to them.
LUKE 24:50

Bible readers will know Bethany as the town where Jesus spent time with His friends Mary, Martha, and Lazarus. Bethany was about two miles from Jerusalem, on the Mount of Olives. It makes sense that Jesus would spend a lot of time there, as it was close to the city.

Bethany is where Mary, sister of Martha, poured out the perfume on Jesus' feet and wiped them with her hair. It was there that Martha was making a meal for Jesus and His followers and wanted Mary to help. Jesus reminded Martha that Mary was doing the better thing of listening to His preaching, rather than rushing around getting things ready. Bethany is also where Jesus raised Lazarus from the dead with just a few words. And Bethany is where Jesus ascended into heaven.

Learn More: Mark 11:1–11

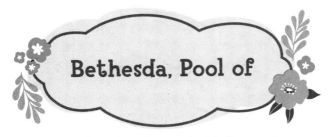

Bethesda, Pool of

*In Jerusalem there is a pool with five porches
called Bethesda near the sheep gate.*
JOHN 5:2

Jesus was in Jerusalem to observe a Jewish holy day when He noticed several sick and disabled people gathered around a pool, the Pool of Bethesda. The people believed an angel came every once in a while to stir the waters, and whoever entered the pool first would be healed.

Although he tried, one man in the group could not get into the water first because his legs did not work properly. Jesus had compassion on the man and healed him with the command "Get up! Pick up your bed and walk" (John 5:8). Because of Jesus' words, the man was healed instantly.

. . . .

Learn More: John 5:1–15

63

Bethlehem

"Bethlehem Ephrathah, you are too little to be among the family groups of Judah. But from you One will come who will rule for Me in Israel. His coming was planned long ago, from the beginning."
MICAH 5:2

Bethlehem is a city that is mentioned many times in both the Old and New Testaments. It was the place that Naomi brought Ruth to after leaving Moab. It is where David tended his sheep in the years before he became king. Hundreds of years before Jesus was born, Micah prophesied that the Messiah would come out of Bethlehem.

That prophecy came true when Caesar Augustus told all the people to return to their hometown to be taxed. Joseph and Mary, mother of Jesus, returned to Bethlehem. That's where Jesus was born on the first Christmas.

Learn More: Matthew 2:1

Calvary

Calvary is a hill just outside the walls of Jerusalem where Jesus was crucified. The word comes from a Latin word meaning "skull," which is why it is called "the Place of the Skull" in John 19:17. The Aramaic word for this place is Golgotha (Mark 15:22).

Jesus carried His own cross partway to Calvary. But He was so weak from being mistreated that the Roman soldiers made a man named Simon help Jesus. Simon carried the cross the rest of the way to the place where Jesus died. He gave His life at Calvary so that we can be forgiven of our sins.

Learn More: Matthew 27:33

PLACES

Cana

This was the first powerful work Jesus did. It was done in Cana of Galilee where He showed His power. His followers put their trust in Him.

JOHN 2:11

Cana is where Jesus' first miracle happened. It is a village about 13 miles west of the Sea of Galilee. Jesus, His disciples, and His mother were all guests at a wedding. Mary, mother of Jesus, told Him about a problem: the host was about to run out of wine to serve the guests! Jesus did not do anything right away because He did not think it was the right time to show His ability to do miracles as the Messiah. But He then gave instructions to the workers to fill jars with water. Jesus turned that ordinary water into wine that was even better than what had been served earlier (John 2:6–10).

Learn More: John 2:1–12

Canaan

"Send men to spy out the land of Canaan which I am going to give to the people of Israel. Send a man from each of their fathers' families, every one a leader among them."
NUMBERS 13:2

PLACES

. . . .

The land of Canaan is also known as the "Promised Land." It was the land the Lord God promised to Abraham, Isaac, and Jacob. After many, many years, the Israelites finally got to move into the land.

Even though Canaan was a small place, it was a part of an important road between Mesopotamia in the north and Egypt to the south. It had a lot of fruit trees and vines, and everything grew well there. The men who had been sent to spy out the area came back and said, "It does flow with milk and honey" (Numbers 13:27).

. . . .

Learn More: Numbers 13

Dead Sea

Then the side of their land went along the north side of Beth-hoglah. And it ended at the north waters of the Salt [Dead] Sea at the south end of the Jordan. This was the south side.
JOSHUA 18:19

The name "Dead Sea" appears only once in the New Life Version of the Bible that we use in this book. It is called the "Salt Sea" in most cases because of the high level of salt found in its water. After the Israelites entered Canaan, this body of water was considered their southern boundary.

The Dead Sea is the Earth's lowest point on land. Its water comes from the Jordan River, but the water does not run out of the sea—it evaporates. The salts and minerals have made its waters almost ten times saltier than regular seawater, and it is a place where no living thing larger than algae can survive. Because there is not much that can live in it, it is known as the Dead Sea.

Learn More: Joshua 3:16

Eden

The Lord God planted a garden to the east in Eden.
He put the man there whom He had made.
GENESIS 2:8

God created the Garden of Eden as a beautiful place where Adam and Eve could enjoy creation and walks with the Lord. The Garden was filled with many beautiful plants and animals. It was a perfect place to be with God and everything He had created.

On a map today, Eden would be somewhere in the region of Mesopotamia near the Tigris and Euphrates rivers. We cannot be sure exactly where it was located, because Adam and Eve were sent out of the Garden after they disobeyed the Lord. The word *Eden* is sometimes used to describe a place of perfection. When God and His people live together again in eternity, it will be Eden!

Learn More: Genesis 2:4–17

Gethsemane

Jesus came with them to a place called Gethsemane. He said to them, "You sit here while I go over there to pray."
MATTHEW 26:36

The Garden of Gethsemane is where Jesus prayed on the night before He was arrested and then crucified. He took His three closest disciples and asked them to pray for Him. Then Jesus went off alone to ask God the Father if there was any way He could avoid what was going to happen. He knew that He would need to face death on the cross to save people from their sins, but the thought of the suffering and death was difficult.

This garden, on the Mount of Olives, is where Jesus prayed for strength to do what He knew He had to do. In Gethsemane, Jesus told His Father that He would do whatever He wanted Him to do. Because of Jesus' sacrifice, we can each have a relationship with Him simply by asking.

Learn More: Matthew 26:36–46

Greece

As he went through those parts of the country, he spoke words of comfort and help to the Christians. Then he went on to the country of Greece.

Acts 20:2

Greece was a powerful, important place in both the Old and New Testaments. The apostle Paul wrote letters to the early Christian churches in the Greek cities of Corinth and Thessalonica.

A man named Alexander the Great conquered much of the world before Paul was born, and he brought Greek culture, customs, and languages to the area around the Mediterranean Sea. Greek became a common language during this time. Paul was able to speak Greek to preach the Gospel of Jesus Christ everywhere he traveled in his missionary journeys.

Learn More: 1 Thessalonians 1

Israel

"Let us thank the Lord God of Israel. He has bought His people and made them free."
Luke 1:68

. . . .

God's people were known as the Israelites, getting their name from their ancestor, Jacob. God gave Jacob the new name of *Israel* because he wrestled with God and men and won.

The nation of Israel divided in two after King Solomon died. Ten tribes in the north were still known as Israel and the two tribes in the south were called Judah. Both Israel and Judah had their own kings. Sadly, Israel had many evil kings who worshipped false gods and led the people away from the one true God. This disobedience and idol worship are the reason that the Israelites were taken captive by Assyria.

. . . .

Learn More: Genesis 32:28

Jericho

PLACES

The Lord said to Joshua, "See, I have given Jericho into your hand, with its king and soldiers."
JOSHUA 6:2

Jericho was the first Canaanite city that the Israelites captured. Moses had died and Joshua became the leader of God's people. The last generation of people died out in the wilderness because of their disobedience. Now a new generation was ready to conquer Canaan and move into the Promised Land.

Jericho was a strong city near the Jordan River. It had thick walls and powerful defenses. God told Joshua to lead the people in a silent march around the city of Jericho for six days. On the seventh day, God told the people to march around the city seven times and then to shout and blow their trumpets. When they made this loud noise, the walls of Jericho collapsed. Because of God's power, the city belonged to the Israelites.

Learn More: Joshua 6

Jerusalem

*May my tongue hold to the roof of my mouth
if I do not remember you, if I do not honor
Jerusalem above my highest joy.*
PSALM 137:6

· ·

Jerusalem was a very special city to the people of Israel. It was their most important place from the time of King David through the life of Jesus. It is still an important city today. Jerusalem is often called the "Holy City" because of its importance to both Jews and Christians.

King David made Jerusalem the capital city of Israel. King Solomon built the temple there. And the Israelites rebuilt Jerusalem after they were released from their captivity in Babylon. We read about Jesus going into Jerusalem for holy days, and He was crucified right outside the city. Today, travelers visit sites around Jerusalem where many believe these events happened.

· ·

Learn More: Matthew 23:37–39

Jordan River

Jesus came to the Jordan River from the town of Nazareth in the country of Galilee. He was baptized by John.
MARK 1:9

The Jordan River runs the whole length of Israel. It starts about 1,500 feet above sea level and flows into the lowest spot on earth, the Dead Sea. This sharp drop is the reason the river was given its name, which means "the descender."

The Jordan River is the place where several miracles in the Old and New Testaments happened. It is where a Syrian army commander named Naaman was healed of his leprosy (2 Kings 5:14) and where God made a path of dry land so the Israelites could cross into the Promised Land (Joshua 3:14–16). In the New Testament, Jesus began His ministry by being baptized in the Jordan River by John the Baptist.

Learn More: Luke 3:21–22

Judah

When Rehoboam came to Jerusalem, he gathered all the family of Judah and the family of Benjamin. He gathered together 180,000 chosen men of war to fight against the family of Israel and return the nation to Rehoboam the son of Solomon.

1 Kings 12:21

Judah is the name of the southern part of Israel that became its own nation after splitting away from the north. While the northern tribes kept the name *Israel*, Judah was made up of two tribes that came from Jacob's sons Judah and Benjamin.

Judah was first ruled by King Solomon's son, Rehoboam. Judah was led by a few good kings and seemed to follow the Lord better than Israel. But Judah also disobeyed God and began to worship idols. The people ignored the messages from God given by prophets like Isaiah and Jeremiah. This disobedience is what caused them to be taken as prisoners by the Babylonians.

Learn More: 2 Chronicles 14:2–8

Kishon River

"I will have Sisera, the head of Jabin's army, meet you at the river Kishon. He will have his war-wagons and his many soldiers with him. But I will give him into your hand."
JUDGES 4:7

God made this promise to Deborah and Barak, the commanders of the Israelite army, who were ready to battle the Canaanites. God made it clear that the Kishon River, a stream in northern Israel, would be an important part of their success.

When the Kishon River overflowed in a sudden rainstorm, Deborah and Barak and their army swooped down on the enemy in the valley. The Canaanite chariots got stuck in the mud, making them an easy target for the Israelite warriors (Judges 4:4–16).

Learn More: Judges 5:21

Mediterranean Sea

The west side of their land was along the side of the Great Sea. These are the sides of the land of the people of Judah by their families.
JOSHUA 15:12

The Great Sea is another name for the Mediterranean Sea. The Mediterranean Sea is the border on the west side of the land of Israel. The tribe of Judah owned the area of land that stretched west to the sea when the land was divided among the tribes. This happened when Joshua was their leader.

The Mediterranean Sea stretched from Israel's coast for about 2,200 miles to the Atlantic Ocean. The Bible mentions other countries that border the Mediterranean Sea: Egypt, Syria, Lebanon, Greece, and Italy.

Learn More: Joshua 23:4

Midian

PLACES

The land of Midian was a desert area near the Dead Sea. It is where Moses made a home for himself after fleeing from Egypt. Moses had killed an Egyptian supervisor while trying to protect a Hebrew slave from punishment. Because of Moses' actions, Pharaoh wanted to capture him, so Moses ran away from Egypt. In Midian, Moses married Zipporah, the daughter of a priest.

While he was looking after his father-in-law's flock of sheep, Moses heard God speaking to him from a burning bush. God told Moses to return to Egypt and lead the Hebrew people to the Promised Land.

Learn More: Exodus 18:1–12

Nazareth

Jesus came to Nazareth where He had grown up.
As He had done before, He went into the Jewish place
of worship on the Day of Rest. Then He stood up to read.
LUKE 4:16

Nazareth was a small town where Jesus grew up. Many people thought poorly of Nazareth. A disciple of Jesus, Philip, once invited a friend to come to see Jesus of Nazareth, the Messiah. Nathanael responded, "Can anything good come out of the town of Nazareth?" (John 1:46).

Even though it was just a small, unpopular village during Jesus' time, Nazareth has grown to be the largest city in Israel's northern district. Christians travel from all over the world to visit Nazareth, to see the city where Jesus grew up.

Learn More: Mark 6:1–6

Nile River

"The Nile will be full of frogs. They will come up and go in your house and in your room and on your bed. They will come in the houses of your servants and on your people. They will come in your stoves and in your bread dough."

EXODUS 8:3

The Nile River is the longest river in Africa and the second-longest river in the world. It gets its water from different sources in East Africa and empties into the Mediterranean Sea.

Most of the references to the Nile are found in the book of Exodus. The Nile is where Moses' mother hid him in a basket to save his life. When Moses was an adult, he proved to Pharaoh that the one true God was more powerful than their Egyptian gods through the plagues that God sent. Several of these plagues took place around the Nile, like the time huge numbers of frogs appeared. The Egyptians worshipped the river for the way it gave life. But they didn't realize it was the Almighty God who created the Nile and provided the water for them.

Learn More: Exodus 7:14–25

Nineveh

"Get up and go to the large city of Nineveh, and preach against it. For their sin has come up before Me."
JONAH 1:2

. . . .

Nineveh was the capital city of Assyria. God told the prophet Jonah to warn the Ninevites of His coming judgment. But Jonah traveled in the opposite direction, getting on a boat in the Mediterranean Sea. These people of Nineveh were enemies of the Israelites and were known for being evil and violent. So Jonah was afraid to go anywhere near Nineveh.

After being swallowed and spit out by a giant fish, Jonah finally obeyed God. He preached a warning message to the city. Amazingly, the people believed Jonah and stopped their wicked behavior. But Jonah was angry that they would not be punished for the evil things they had done, and he asked God why they shouldn't be in trouble. The Lord reminded Jonah that He was a loving God who shows mercy even to people who have been very evil. If they turn to God, He will forgive.

. . . .

Learn More: Jonah 3

Persia

PLACES

All the acts of his power and strength, and the whole story of the high honor given to Mordecai by the king, are written in the Book of the Chronicles of the kings of Media and Persia.
ESTHER 10:2

Persia was the kingdom that conquered Babylon. This made it possible for the Jewish exiles to return home to Jerusalem. Then they could rebuild their city and temple.

We read in the Old Testament about several Persian kings who helped God's people and protected them. King Cyrus gave back all the things that had been taken from the temple by King Nebuchadnezzar of Babylon. King Darius became friends with Daniel and praised God when Daniel was saved from the lions' den. King Ahasuerus married Esther, a Jew, and made her the queen in Persia. Persia's capital city was Susa, where the prophet Daniel had visions of great world empires and the future Messiah (Daniel 8:2).

Learn More: Ezra 9:9

Red Sea

*So God led the people through the desert to
get to the Red Sea. The people of Israel went
out of the land of Egypt ready for war.*
EXODUS 13:18

In the book of Exodus, we read that after ten plagues against Egypt, Pharaoh finally let the Israelites leave Egypt. But they had not gotten very far before Pharaoh changed his mind. He sent his army to capture the people and bring them back again.

God commanded Moses to lift his staff (a kind of walking stick), and when he did, God divided the sea in half. Moses led the people across dry land between two walls of water! When all of the Israelites had made it safely across, God let the water close back in, destroying the Egyptian army.

Learn More: Exodus 14

Sea of Galilee

*Jesus was walking by the Sea of Galilee. He saw
Simon and his brother Andrew putting a
net into the sea. They were fishermen.*
MARK 1:16

Many miracles from Jesus' ministry take place on or around the Sea of Galilee. It is where He called His first disciples, Peter and Andrew, to leave their fishing nets and follow Him. It is also where He healed many people who came to Him and where He fed 5,000 people with one boy's lunch.

On the Sea of Galilee, Jesus calmed a storm that came up while He and His disciples were on a boat. He also walked on water to His disciples' boat and called to Peter to walk on the water too. Peter did fine until he took his eyes off Jesus, then he sank. But Jesus reached out and saved him!

Learn More: John 6:1–27

Sinai, Mount

When the Lord had finished speaking with Moses on Mount Sinai, He gave him the two stone writings of the Law, pieces of stone written on by the finger of God.
EXODUS 31:18

. . . .

Mount Sinai is also known in the Bible by another name, Mount Horeb. It is here that Moses met with God, who spoke through a burning bush. Later, Moses would meet with the Lord again when he received the Ten Commandments, which explained how the people of Israel should honor God with their lives.

Sinai is also the place the prophet Elijah ran to when he needed a place to escape Queen Jezebel's anger.

. . . .

Learn More: Exodus 24:12–18

Zarephath

"Get up and go to Zarephath, which belongs to Sidon, and stay there. I have told a woman there, whose husband has died, to feed you."
1 KINGS 17:9

Zarephath was a city on the coast of the Mediterranean Sea. This is the town where Elijah was sent after he announced God's prophecy of drought and famine in the land. God told Elijah that He would provide for him if he went to the home of a certain widow. This woman only had a small amount of oil and flour that would not even be enough for herself and her son. But, showing great faith, she made some bread for Elijah. Then God took care of all of them by never allowing her supply of oil and flour to run out.

Learn More: 1 Kings 17:8–16

Fall of Satan

"How you have fallen from heaven, O shining one, son of the morning! You have been cut down to the earth, you who have made the nations weak!"
ISAIAH 14:12

EVENTS

Before the creation of the earth, we know that there were heavenly beings—angels—who worshipped the Lord. But one of the angels became full of pride and didn't want to worship God. He wanted to be worshipped! This angel was called Lucifer, and he and one-third of the angels were sent away from heaven and the presence of God for their rebellion.

After their "fall" from heaven, they are now known as Satan and his demons.

Learn More: Revelation 12:7–9

Creation of Man and Woman

And God made man in His own likeness. In the likeness of God He made him. He made both male and female.
GENESIS 1:27

God spent five days creating the universe—the earth and stars, the sun and moon, the birds, fish, and animals. On day six, God created Adam to take care of the earth and all that was in it. God wanted other beings to enjoy Him and share in His nature. So He made Adam by taking dust from the ground, forming him, and then breathing His very own life into man.

Adam was made to have a relationship with God and to take care of the earth. God didn't want Adam to be alone on the earth, though, so He created a woman to be Adam's partner. She was given the name Eve.

Learn More: Genesis 2

Temptation of Eve

The woman saw that the tree was good for food, and pleasing to the eyes, and could fill the desire of making one wise. So she took of its fruit and ate. She also gave some to her husband, and he ate.

GENESIS 3:6

EVENTS

Adam and Eve walked with God and enjoyed all of the wonderful things He created. God said they could eat from any tree in the Garden of Eden except for one tree, the Tree of Knowledge of Good and Evil. One day, as they were in the garden, a snake spoke to Eve and tricked her into thinking that God was keeping a secret from her and Adam.

The snake—who was really Satan—said if Adam and Eve ate from the Tree of Knowledge, they would be like God. The serpent told Eve that God's warning was false—that she wouldn't really die if she disobeyed. So Eve ate the fruit and gave some to Adam, and they immediately knew they had sinned against God. Because of their disobedience, sin became a part of the world, ruining their perfect relationship with Him.

Learn More: Genesis 3

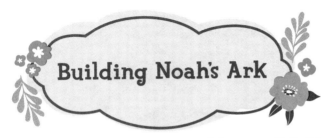

Building Noah's Ark

"Make a large boat of gopher wood for yourself. Build rooms in the boat. And cover it inside and out with tar."
GENESIS 6:14

. . . .

Adam and Eve had sinned many years before. People were born in sin and did many sinful things. God saw how bad everyone had become and He decided to destroy the whole earth.

But God also saw that Noah was still obeying Him. So God told Noah to build a very large boat because a huge rain would soon flood the whole earth. At that time, there had never been any rain before! Noah obeyed God and built the boat, also called the ark. It would be a safe home for him and his family, as well as two of each kind of animal and bird, during the flood.

. . . .

Learn More: Genesis 6

EVENTS

The Flood

The flood came upon the earth for forty days.
The water got deeper and raised up the large
boat so that it was lifted above the earth.
GENESIS 7:17

The ark was built. The supplies were loaded. The animals were on board. Then Noah and his family sat inside the ship for seven days, waiting for the end. Their wicked neighbors must have had a good time making fun of them.

At the end of the week, the waters came suddenly. The Bible says that the wells of water under the earth broke open and the windows of heaven were opened. The storm lasted for 40 days and 40 nights.

When the storm stopped and the water dried up, the ark came to rest on Mount Ararat. Noah, his family, and all of the animals and birds got off the ark. The people gave thanks to God for the way He took care of them.

Learn More: Genesis 8:13–22

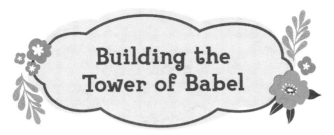

Building the Tower of Babel

So the name of the city was Babel, because there the Lord mixed up the language of the whole earth. The Lord sent the people everywhere over the whole earth.

GENESIS 11:9

. . . .

After Noah's family left the ark, they began to have children, and the number of people on the earth grew larger. The people all spoke one language and wanted to stay together in one place instead of spreading across the earth as God instructed them. They decided they would build a tower to heaven to make themselves famous.

God saw what they were doing and took away their ability to speak the same language. The people, who were suddenly unable to understand each other, moved out across the land with others who spoke their same new language.

. . . .

Learn More: Genesis 11:1–9

Birth of Isaac

*Abraham gave the name Isaac to his
son who was born to him by Sarah.*
GENESIS 21:3

God saw Abraham's faith and promised him that he would have a son with Sarah. God also promised that Abraham would have so many descendants that they could not be counted. He said that Sarah would give birth to a son and they were to name him Isaac.

God's promise came true. When Abraham was 100 years old, he became father to the promised son. Isaac's name means "laughter," and his birth brought much joy to Abraham and Sarah. Sarah had even laughed at God's promise to give her a son in her old age. Isaac's birth is just another reminder that God always keeps His promises to us, even when they seem unbelievable!

Learn More: Genesis 21:1–8

Isaac Is Nearly Sacrificed

The angel of the Lord said, "Do not put out your hand against the boy. Do nothing to him. For now I know that you fear God. You have not kept from Me your son, your only son."
GENESIS 22:12

One day God called, "Abraham!"

He replied, "Here I am" (Genesis 22:1). God then told him to take his son Isaac and sacrifice him on Mount Moriah. Abraham was stunned. But he trusted in God and set out for the mountain with his promised son.

Abraham was willing to prove his faith in God and sacrifice Isaac as God said. Just as Abraham prepared to kill Isaac, though, the angel of the Lord stopped him. God provided a ram—a male sheep—as the sacrifice instead of Isaac. Because of Abraham's faith, God promised that good would come to Abraham and to the whole world through his family.

Learn More: Genesis 22:1–19

Jacob Wrestles with God

And the man said, "Your name will no longer be Jacob, but Israel. For you have fought with God and with men, and have won."
GENESIS 32:28

EVENTS

Jacob had run away from his twin brother, Esau, after tricking Esau out of his inheritance and blessing. He spent many years living in another land. There, he got married and had children, as well as gaining much livestock. But after a while, he wanted to return home.

On his journey back to meet his brother, Jacob and a man wrestled all through the night. When Jacob realized that it was not just a man he was wrestling, but God Himself, he said he would not stop wrestling until the "man" blessed him.

God did bless Jacob. And God changed his name to "Israel," which would later be the name of God's special people.

Learn More: Genesis 32:22–32

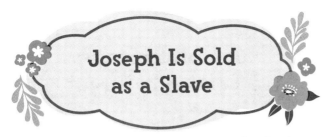

Joseph Is Sold as a Slave

Some Midianite traders were passing by. So the brothers pulled Joseph up out of the hole. And they sold him to the Ishmaelites for twenty pieces of silver, and they took Joseph to Egypt.
GENESIS 37:28

Joseph, son of Jacob, was born to his father's favorite wife, Rachel. Joseph was Jacob's favorite. He got special treatment, including the gift of a colorful coat.

Joseph often told his father when his older brothers were doing wrong. So his brothers hated him. He also told his family the dreams he had about them all bowing down to him. Joseph's brothers came up with a plan to get rid of him.

One day, Joseph was checking up on his brothers, far from their father's camp. The older boys took Joseph's special coat from him and threw him into an empty water pit. Then they sold him to some traveling merchants. The merchants took Joseph to Egypt, where he became a slave.

Learn More: Genesis 37:12–36

Joseph Becomes a Leader in Egypt

Joseph said to them, "Do not the meanings of dreams belong to God? Tell them to me."
GENESIS 40:8

EVENTS

It was bad enough that Joseph, son of Jacob, became a slave in Egypt. Then when someone lied about him, he became a prisoner too!

One night, two other prisoners had dreams, and God helped Joseph to explain them. When the king of Egypt, Pharaoh, had some strange dreams, Joseph was called in to interpret them too. He did, telling Pharaoh that the dreams meant a time of famine was coming. Food would be very hard to find unless Egypt saved up food during the good years.

God told Joseph there would be seven years of good harvests before the famine. Pharaoh made an important decision: Joseph would be in charge of Egypt to prepare for the coming disaster!

Learn More: Genesis 41:1–43

The Israelites Move to Egypt

"I am God, the God of your father. Do not be afraid to go to Egypt. For I will make you a great nation there."
GENESIS 46:3

The famine that Joseph, son of Jacob, had predicted happened in Egypt and nearby countries. Joseph's own brothers, who had sold him into slavery, needed food. When they heard there was plenty of food in Egypt, they traveled there to buy some.

They were shocked and scared to learn that the powerful man selling the food was the little brother they had treated so badly. But Joseph forgave them and told them that God had used their bad behavior to save many lives. Joseph sent them back to their home with food. And he urged them to come back to live in Egypt, along with their father, Jacob. For years, he thought his favorite son was dead. Now, as a very old man, Jacob would get to see Joseph again!

Learn More: Genesis 46:26–30

EVENTS

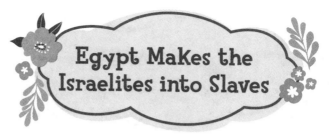

Egypt Makes the Israelites into Slaves

A new king came into power over Egypt. He did not know Joseph.
EXODUS 1:8

- -

EVENTS

Joseph, son of Jacob, was such a wise, good man that Pharaoh trusted him to lead the whole country. Joseph's family was welcomed in Egypt, where they had many babies and grew into a big, strong family.

But after Joseph died, a new king took over. He didn't know Joseph and thought Joseph's family—the Israelites—were a problem. So the new pharaoh decided to make the Israelites into slaves. He put soldiers over them to make them work hard building cities for Egypt.

The people cried out to God because their lives were so hard. God loved His people and felt sorry for them. So He made a plan to rescue them with a man named Moses.

- -

Learn More: Exodus 1:1–14

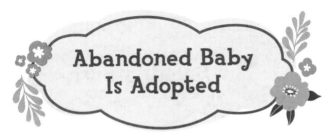

Abandoned Baby Is Adopted

The child grew, and she brought him to
Pharaoh's daughter. And he became her
son. She gave him the name Moses, saying,
"Because I took him out of the water."
EXODUS 2:10

After Joseph, son of Jacob, invited his family to Egypt to save them from a famine in the land, their family grew. They were made to be slaves in Egypt. But eventually there were so many Hebrews that the pharaoh was afraid they would try to take his land from him. He commanded that baby boys be thrown into the Nile River.

A certain Hebrew couple could not do this, though, and they hid their newborn baby boy. His mother put him in a basket and made sure the basket was placed in the tall grass beside the river. Pharaoh's daughter came to bathe in the river and found the basket. She adopted the baby as her own and named him Moses, which means "taken out of the water."

Learn More: Exodus 2:1–10

EVENTS

The Burning Bush

*There the Angel of the Lord showed Himself to Moses
in a burning fire from inside a bush. Moses looked
and saw that the bush was burning with fire,
but it was not being burned up.*

EXODUS 3:2

EVENTS

Moses left Egypt as a young man and then spent 40 years as a shepherd, taking care of his father-in-law's flock. One day, he saw a strange sight: a bush was on fire, but it wasn't burning up! He stepped in for a closer look.

That's when God spoke out of the burning bush and told Moses that He was the God of all and that He had an important job for Moses to do. God wanted Moses to go to Egypt to save His people from their slavery.

Moses had grown up as the grandson of Egypt's king, the pharaoh. But he did not feel important enough to do the job that God was calling him to do. The Lord promised Moses that He would always be with him and would help him.

Learn More: Exodus 3:1–12

Ten Plagues on Egypt

*"Pharaoh will not listen to you. Then I will lay My hand
on Egypt. By great acts that will punish the Egyptians,
I will bring out My family groups, My people,
the sons of Israel, from the land of Egypt."*
EXODUS 7:4

Moses took his brother, Aaron, with him to ask Pharaoh
to free the Israelites. God had told Moses that Pharaoh
would not let the people go until he saw God's power.

Moses and Aaron used their staffs (walking sticks)
to bring ten plagues against the Egyptians. "Plagues"
are terrible troubles, things like the Nile River turning
to blood; frogs, lice, and flies covering the land; and the
death of all the Egyptians' cows. Then came a plague of
painful boils on the Egyptians, a hailstorm, a swarm of
locusts that ate all of the Egyptian crops, and darkness
that covered the land. But Pharaoh still refused to let
God's people go. The last plague was that all the firstborn of the Egyptian families died. Pharaoh's son was
one of those who died, and Pharaoh finally let the
Israelites go.

Learn More: Exodus 7:1–11:10

God Parts the Red Sea

"Lift up your special stick and put out your hand over the sea, and divide it. Then the people of Israel will go through the sea on dry land."
EXODUS 14:16

EVENTS

The Israelites thought Pharaoh really wanted them to leave Egypt. But as they came close to the Red Sea, they realized Pharaoh had sent his army to capture them. They couldn't escape because they were trapped by the sea!

But God had a plan. He told Moses to lift his staff, and God sent a strong wind to blow the waters apart. The water turned into walls on both sides of a dry path. The Israelites crossed the sea on dry land. The Egyptians caught up to them and tried to follow them through the sea, but the Lord let the water fall back on them. The whole Egyptian army drowned. The Israelites were safe!

Learn More: Exodus 14

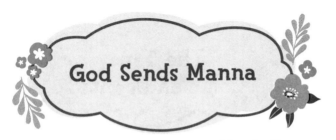

God Sends Manna

*Then the Lord said to Moses, "See, I will
rain bread from heaven for you."*
EXODUS 16:4

After the Israelites had traveled in the desert for several
weeks, they ran out of food. They complained to Moses,
saying that God brought them to the desert to die from
hunger. But God promised that He would rain down
bread from heaven.

The Lord sent this bread every morning. It was like
dew on the grass. The people would gather what they
needed for the day. They called the bread *manna* because that means "what is it?" They ate the manna for
40 years until they came to Canaan, the land God had
promised them.

Learn More: Exodus 16:4–36

The Ten Commandments

When the Lord had finished speaking with Moses on Mount Sinai, He gave him the two stone writings of the Law, pieces of stone written on by the finger of God.
EXODUS 31:18

EVENTS

God asked Moses to go to Mount Sinai. The Lord spent 40 days there with Moses, giving him the laws for God's people. At the end of the 40 days, He gave Moses ten commandments written on stone tablets by His hand. These were laws such as "Do not have gods other than Me," "Do not make false idols," and "Do not take the Lord's name in vain." The Israelites were also commanded to rest and worship God on the Sabbath and to honor their parents, and not to commit murder, steal, lie, break their marriage vows, or covet (to want the things another person has).

Learn More: Exodus 20:1–17

Twelve Spies Report on Canaan

Moses sent them to spy out the land of Canaan.
He said to them, "Go up there into the Negev.
Then go up into the hill country."
NUMBERS 13:17

When the Israelites came to the edge of the Promised Land, Moses chose one young man from each of the twelve tribes to go into the land. Their job was to find out if they could conquer it.

The men were in Canaan for 40 days. When they returned to Moses, they all reported that the land was beautiful and full of good food. But ten men said they could *not* conquer the land because there were giants living there. Caleb and Joshua were the only two who believed the Lord would give the land to them.

As punishment for Israel's disobedience, God said that none of the people, except Joshua and Caleb, would be allowed to enter the Promised Land.

Learn More: Numbers 13:1–14:38

Rahab Spares the Spies

And she [Rahab] said to the men, "I know that the Lord has given you the land. The fear of you has come upon us. All the people living in the land have become weak with fear because of you."
JOSHUA 2:9

EVENTS

Joshua, preparing for their first battle for the Promised Land, sent two spies into the city of Jericho. These spies tried to escape being noticed by going to the home of a woman named Rahab who lived on the city wall. Even though they tried to be secretive, someone reported them and soldiers came, looking for the spies. Rahab knew they were God's people, though, and hid them on her roof under bundles of grain.

When it was safe to help them escape, she asked that they spare her family when they came to take over Jericho. They promised her that her family would be saved from harm. Rahab had acted in faith, and it saved her and her family.

Learn More: Joshua 2:1–21

Jericho's Walls Collapse

So the people called out and the religious leaders blew the horns. When the people heard the sound of the horns, they called out even louder. And the wall fell to the ground. All the people went straight in and took the city.

JOSHUA 6:20

The people of Jericho were not afraid of the Israelites. They felt safe behind the thick walls of their city. Jericho's residents believed nobody could break through them.

God spoke with Joshua and gave him some strange instructions. For six days Joshua's army, carrying the ark of the covenant, was to walk quietly around Jericho, once a day. On the seventh day, they were to walk around the city seven times. When the priests sounded a long blast on the trumpets, the army was to shout. Then the city walls would fall!

It took a lot of faith to believe this plan would work, but Joshua believed. They obeyed God's instructions, and the mighty walls of Jericho came crashing down.

Learn More: Joshua 6

EVENTS

Deborah Goes to Battle

Now Lappidoth's wife Deborah, a woman who spoke for God, was judging Israel at that time.
JUDGES 4:4

· ·

While the Israelites were becoming a nation, before they had a king, God sent them "judges" to protect them. These judges were meant to save the people from their enemies.

One time, God chose a woman named Deborah to judge Israel. In a time of war, she talked with the commander Barak. She told him that if he gathered an army on Mount Tabor near the Kishon River, God would make the Canaanites come to them. Then God would give the Israelites victory in battle. Barak knew that Deborah was a wise prophet and military commander, so he told her he would go only if she went with him. Deborah agreed. God sent a sudden downpour of rain that overflowed the river and swept away the Canaanite army. The Israelite army easily captured those who had not been swept away in the flood.

· ·

Learn More: Judges 4

The Downfall of Samson

Samson said, "Let me die with the Philistines!" Then he pushed with all his strength so that the building fell on the leaders and all the people in it. He killed more at his death than he killed in his life.
JUDGES 16:30

Samson was a judge in Israel who was known for being very strong. God gave him this strength because of Samson's obedience in not cutting his hair. Then Samson fell in love with Delilah, who did not obey God. The enemy Philistines had promised her a reward if she would find out the source of Samson's strength. After asking him over and over again, she finally learned that his long hair was the reason he was strong. Delilah called a man to cut off Samson's hair while he slept, and the Philistines captured him. They made Samson blind and forced him to work for them by grinding grain.

During a big feast, the Philistines brought Samson out to make fun of him. But God gave Samson strength one last time. He pushed down the pillars of the temple, causing the roof to fall in and destroy the Philistines inside.

Learn More: Judges 16

Samuel Anoints David

Then Samuel took the horn of oil and poured the oil on him in front of his brothers. The Spirit of the Lord came upon David with strength from that day on.
1 SAMUEL 16:13

EVENTS

After the judges, Israel wanted a king. The prophet Samuel didn't think that was a good idea, but God told him to anoint a tall, good-looking man named Saul. Before long, King Saul was making choices that went against God. The Lord told the prophet to stop feeling bad about it and go to Bethlehem. God had chosen a new king.

A man named Jesse and his sons had come to offer a sacrifice. When Samuel saw Eliab, Jesse's tall, handsome, oldest son, he thought he would make a good king. But God told Samuel, "The Lord does not look at the things man looks at. A man looks at the outside of a person, but the Lord looks at the heart" (1 Samuel 16:7). David was Jesse's youngest son and looked the least like a king. But when he arrived, God told Samuel to anoint him as king.

Learn More: 1 Samuel 16:1–13

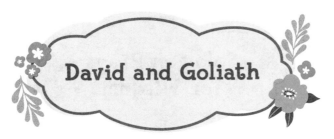

David and Goliath

*So David won the fight against the
Philistine with a sling and a stone.*
1 SAMUEL 17:50

. . . .

The Philistines were in a battle against the Israelites.
Goliath, a Philistine giant, marched forward and dared
any Israelite soldier to fight him. For 40 days, no Israelite
dared step forward.

One day, David came to deliver food to his brothers,
who were in the army. When he heard Goliath's challenge,
he asked for permission to fight, and King Saul said yes.
David shouted to Goliath, "You come to me with a sword
and spears. But I come to you in the name of the Lord of
All" (1 Samuel 17:45). David wasn't wearing battle armor
but rushed toward the giant fighter anyway. As he ran,
he swung his sling and sent a stone slamming into the
giant's forehead. Goliath fell to the ground, and David
cut his head off! The Philistine army fled, and God gave
the Israelites a great victory.

. . . .

Learn More: 1 Samuel 1

Solomon Prays for Wisdom

"So give Your servant an understanding heart to judge Your people and know the difference between good and bad. For who is able to judge Your many people?"
1 KINGS 3:9

EVENTS

David was king for 40 years. He made some mistakes, but he was known as "a man after God's own heart." When he was close to dying, David said his son Solomon should be the next king.

As a young man, Solomon loved the Lord and obeyed all His commandments. One night while he was sleeping, God appeared to Solomon in a dream and said, "Ask what you wish Me to give you" (1 Kings 3:5). Solomon could have asked for money or to win every battle. Instead, he asked that he would be a wise king. This answer pleased God.

The Lord gave Solomon what he asked for, making him wiser than any other man on earth. And because he didn't ask for anything selfishly, God also gave Solomon what he had not asked for—great riches, honor, and peace in his kingdom.

Learn More: 1 Kings 3:1–15

Israel Divides

*All Israel saw that the king did not listen to them.
So they said to the king, "What share do we have
in David? We have no share in the son of Jesse!
To your tents, O Israel! Now look after your own
house, David!" So Israel went to their tents.*
1 KINGS 12:16

King Solomon started well but then made some terrible choices. He married 700 women, and they caused him to worship false gods.

After Solomon died, Israel gathered to make his son Rehoboam king. But they asked Rehoboam to be easier on them than Solomon had been. He had made them work hard and charged them high taxes.

Rehoboam got some bad advice and told the people he would be even tougher than his father had been. So ten northern tribes broke away to form their own nation. These tribes kept the name Israel, while two southern tribes—Judah and Benjamin—started a new nation called Judah. Israel and Judah would argue and fight against each other for hundreds of years.

Learn More: 1 Kings 11:26–12:24

EVENTS

Miracle of the Widow's Oil

When the jars were full, she said to her son, "Bring me another jar." And he said to her, "There is not one jar left." Then the oil stopped flowing.
2 KINGS 4:6

Many prophets followed Elisha and learned from him. When one of these prophets passed away suddenly, his family was left without any money. So that man's widow went to Elisha to ask for help. The prophet had owed money to another man, who was coming to take away this widow's sons as payment!

Elisha asked what she had in her house. The woman was down to just one jar of oil. Elisha told her to collect jars from all of her neighbors. He then told her to pour her oil into the jars she'd gathered. She obeyed, and the oil kept flowing until all the empty jars were filled! Elisha then told her to sell the oil, pay her debt, and keep the leftover money for her expenses.

Learn More: 2 Kings 4:1–7

Jonah Runs Away

Jonah paid money, and got on the ship to
go with them, to get away from the Lord.
JONAH 1:3

The Assyrians were the most violent, cruel empire the world had ever seen. So at first the prophet Jonah was happy when God told him that its capital city, Nineveh, would be destroyed if they did not repent. But he was scared to go and deliver God's message that they would be punished for their sins. So Jonah took a ship to Tarshish, trying to run away from God.

On the voyage, God sent a storm, the sailors threw Jonah overboard, he was swallowed by a big fish, and was spit up on the shore. Once again he was told to go warn Nineveh, but this time he obeyed.

Jonah was angry that Nineveh had a second chance. He believed they should pay for their sins. But God showed His mercy and did not destroy them, because they stopped their sinful ways.

Learn More: Jonah 1–4

Israel and Judah Are Destroyed

Then they burned the house of God, and broke down the wall of Jerusalem. They burned all of its buildings built for battles, and destroyed all of its objects of great worth.
2 CHRONICLES 36:19

For many years, God's people lived in two nations, Israel and Judah. The kings of Israel were very bad and led the people to worship false gods. God was very unhappy with this. Even though He warned them through His prophets, the people refused to obey. Finally, as punishment, God allowed the evil Assyrians to overrun Israel.

The kings of Judah were a little better. Some of them followed God and led the people to do the same. But overall Judah had many of the same problems as Israel did. God's prophets urged the people to turn from their sins and follow God with all their hearts. But in time, God allowed the Babylonians to destroy Judah and its capital city of Jerusalem. Many people were taken away as prisoners, forced to live in exile in Babylon.

Learn More: 2 Kings 25:1–21

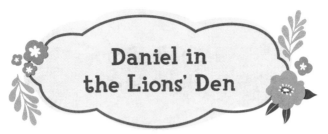

Daniel in the Lions' Den

Then the king was very pleased and had Daniel taken up out of the hole in the ground. So they took Daniel out of the hole and saw that he had not been hurt at all, because he had trusted in his God.

DANIEL 6:23

Daniel was a young man from Judah taken away into exile. Because he honored God in all he did, Daniel became an important leader in the government of Babylon and Persia. This made many of the other leaders jealous. So they got King Darius to make a law that no one could pray to any god for 30 days—only to the king. Anyone who disobeyed should be thrown into the lions' den. Darius agreed, and it became law.

Daniel continued praying faithfully to God. When the leaders told King Darius about Daniel breaking the law, the king was sad. But he could not undo the law. Darius had Daniel thrown into the lions' den.

The next morning, the king called to Daniel, asking if he was still alive. Daniel told him yes—God had sent an angel to shut the lions' mouths. He was safe!

Learn More: Daniel 6

EVENTS

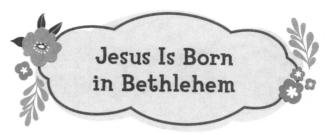

Jesus Is Born in Bethlehem

Her first son was born. She put cloth around Him and laid Him in a place where cattle are fed. There was no room for them in the place where people stay for the night.
LUKE 2:7

Many years after Daniel, the Roman Empire ruled the lands of the Bible. The leader, Caesar Augustus, announced that the entire Roman world would be taxed. Everyone had to return to their family's hometown. A couple named Joseph and Mary, descendants of King David, had to travel to Bethlehem. Mary was pregnant as they made the journey.

When they arrived, the town was full of people who had also come to register. There was no place for them to stay. Mary, mother of Jesus, took shelter in a cave that served as an animal stable. That's where Jesus was born.

Shepherds were watching their flocks in the hills nearby. An angel appeared to them, telling them the good news that the Messiah was born. A huge number of angels suddenly appeared, and they were praising God. The shepherds were amazed. They quickly left their flocks and went to find Jesus to worship Him.

Learn More: Luke 2:1–20

Visit of the Wise Men

They [the wise men] went into the house and found the young Child with Mary, His mother. Then they got down before Him and worshiped Him. They opened their bags of riches and gave Him gifts of gold and perfume and spices.

MATTHEW 2:11

Wise men who lived in Persia saw a new, bright star in the skies and were certain it meant a great king had been born in Israel. They traveled to Jerusalem, and when they arrived, they went to King Herod's palace. They asked, "Where is the King of the Jews Who has been born? We have seen His star in the East. We have come to worship Him" (Matthew 2:2).

Herod was worried that this new king would take his power away from him. He told the wise men to go to Bethlehem and search for the child, then come back and tell him where they found Him. The wise men found Jesus, gave Him gifts, and worshipped Him. But they did not go back to King Herod, who really wanted to *kill* Jesus. God had warned them about returning to tell him that they had found the baby king.

Learn More: Matthew 2:1–12

The Devil Tempts Jesus

Jesus was led by the Holy Spirit to a desert.
There He was tempted by the devil.
MATTHEW 4:1

EVENTS

When Jesus was around 30 years old, after He was baptized by John the Baptist, the Holy Spirit led Him into the desert. Jesus fasted (He did not eat) for 40 days. Then the devil tempted Him, saying, "If You are the Son of God, tell these stones to be made into bread" (Matthew 4:3). The devil also tried to get Jesus to do other things He shouldn't. But Jesus always does the right thing, so Satan lost.

The devil wasn't trying to make Jesus doubt that He was God's Son. Jesus knew who He was. Satan was trying to tempt Jesus to use His power for selfish reasons. But that's not why Jesus had come. He had come down from heaven, not to do His own will, but to do the will of the Father who sent Him. Jesus stayed true to His mission, to die on the cross for the sins of all people.

Learn More: Matthew 4:1–11

Jesus Calls Fishermen

Jesus said to them, "Follow Me.
I will make you fish for men!"
MARK 1:17

After Jesus was tempted by the devil in the wilderness, He went to the town of Capernaum. There, He began preaching, and people began to follow Him. One day, as He walked by the Sea of Galilee, Jesus saw two brothers, Peter and Andrew. Jesus called out to them and told them to leave their fishing nets to follow Him. They immediately dropped their nets to follow Him.

Jesus then saw James and John the apostle mending nets in their boat with their father. He called out the same invitation to them: "Follow Me. I will make you fish for men!" (Matthew 4:19). James and John left their boat and their dad and became disciples of Jesus too.

Learn More: Matthew 4:18–22

EVENTS

Jesus Calms a Storm

He got up and spoke sharp words to the wind. He said to the sea, "Be quiet! Be still." At once the wind stopped blowing. There were no more waves.
MARK 4:39

After a long day of preaching the Good News, Jesus told His disciples to take the boat over to the other side of the Sea of Galilee. While they were heading to the other side, Jesus fell asleep in the back of the boat. As He was sleeping, a big storm came up and the boat began to fill with water.

The disciples were very afraid that the storm would make the boat sink. So they woke Jesus up. He wasn't afraid though. Jesus spoke directly to the wind and the waves and commanded them to be still. The storm obeyed immediately.

Jesus asked His disciples why they were so scared and why they didn't have faith. They didn't understand how the wind and waves obeyed Him. But they would learn over time to have more faith in Jesus.

Learn More: Mark 4:35–41

A Miracle Feeds a Huge Crowd

They all ate and were filled. They picked up twelve baskets full of pieces of bread and fish after the people were finished eating.
MATTHEW 14:20

Jesus heard that John the Baptist had been killed by King Herod. The Lord was sad and wanted to be alone for a while, so He took a boat to get away for some time by Himself. The crowds found out where He was going, though and followed Him. Jesus made time for the people and healed the ones who were sick.

The disciples wanted Jesus to send the people back home since nobody had enough food. But Jesus took the only food they could find—five loaves of bread and two fish—blessed it, and broke it into pieces. His disciples passed the food around and it was enough for everyone, 5,000 men plus women and children. There were even twelve baskets left over!

Learn More: Matthew 14:13–21

Jesus Walks on Water

*Just before the light of day, Jesus went
to them walking on the water.*
MATTHEW 14:25

After feeding a large crowd of people, Jesus sent the disciples away on a boat and went by Himself to a mountain to pray. Alone when evening came, He saw the disciples' boat across the water. It was being tossed around by the waves in a storm.

As the dawn arrived, Jesus walked toward the disciples' boat, on top of the water! The disciples were afraid. They thought Jesus was a ghost. How could a person walk on water?

But Peter bravely asked to join Jesus, and Jesus said, "Come!" Peter walked on the water to Him, but when he took his eyes off Jesus, he quickly sank. Jesus reached out and saved him though. Then they got back into the boat and the storm calmed down. The disciples worshipped Jesus and recognized that He was the Son of God.

Learn More: Matthew 14:22–33

Messiah Enters Jerusalem

They said, "Great and honored is the King Who comes in the name of the Lord. There is peace and greatness in the highest heaven."
LUKE 19:38

After about three years of teaching and preaching and healing people, Jesus went to Jerusalem for the last time. Crowds who knew of His many miracles—including raising Lazarus from the dead—rushed out to meet Him. Jesus sent two disciples to the village ahead and had them bring back a donkey and her colt. This fulfilled an Old Testament prophecy: "See, your King is coming to you. He is fair and good and has the power to save. He is not proud and sits on a donkey" (Zechariah 9:9).

The crowd spread their coats and branches from the trees on the road for Jesus to ride on. As He entered Jerusalem, the entire city was caught up in the excitement. They thought Jesus would bring a change in the government and get rid of the hated Romans. But Jesus was coming to bring a change to people's hearts.

Learn More: Matthew 21:1–11

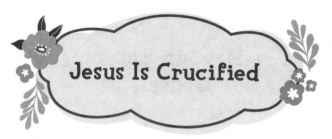

Jesus Is Crucified

When they came to the place called Calvary,
they nailed Jesus to a cross. The other two men
were nailed to crosses also. One was on the right
side of Jesus and the other was on His left side.
LUKE 23:33

The religious leaders hated Jesus. They knew He was popular with the people, and He often pointed out their selfishness and greed. So they worked together to have Him arrested and killed.

They took Jesus to King Herod and then the Roman governor, Pilate. They lied about Jesus because they did not like the miracles He was doing and that He was showing proof that He was the Son of God. Pilate gave the people a choice between letting Jesus or another prisoner free. The people, caught up in the leaders' anger, chose the other prisoner, Barabbas. He was a murderer.

Jesus was sentenced to die on a cross. He carried the cross toward Calvary until He stumbled. Then the soldiers made a man named Simon carry it the rest of the way. Jesus was nailed to the cross and died in pain. Jesus suffered all of this pain in our place so that we can be freed from the punishment for our sin.

Learn More: Luke 23:26–49

Jesus Rises from the Dead

"Do not be afraid. You are looking for Jesus of Nazareth Who was nailed to a cross. He is risen! He is not here! See, here is the place where they laid Him."
MARK 16:6

Jesus had been in the tomb for two days, but on the morning of the third day, the earth shook and an angel of the Lord came down from heaven. He pushed back the stone that blocked the entrance of the tomb. The Roman soldiers guarding it were terrified.

Some of Jesus' friends had come to the tomb to be near His body. But an angel told Mary Magdalene and another woman named Mary that Jesus was no longer there. "He is risen!" the angel said. The women were excited and ran to tell Jesus' other followers. As they were on their way, Jesus met them and proved that He was alive. He told them that they shouldn't be afraid.

Learn More: Matthew 18:1–15

Jesus Appears to Mary Magdalene

After saying this, she turned around and saw Jesus standing there. But she did not know that it was Jesus.
JOHN 20:14

Mary Magdalene told Peter and John the apostle that the stone had been rolled away from Jesus' tomb. She told them that she did not know where His body had been placed. They went back with her to the tomb, saw that it was empty, and believed that Jesus had risen from the dead as He had promised. So they returned home.

Mary stayed at the tomb, crying because she didn't know where her Lord was. Suddenly, Jesus was there with her, asking her why she was crying. She didn't recognize Him at first, but when she did, she ran to tell the others. Jesus told her He needed to go back to the Father in heaven, and then He would return to His followers.

Learn More: John 20:1–18

Jesus Rises Up to Heaven

And while He was praying that good would come to them, He went from them (and was taken up to heaven and they worshiped Him.) Then they went back to Jerusalem with great joy.
LUKE 24:51–52

. . . .

Jesus told His disciples to return to Jerusalem. As they ate together, Jesus commanded them, "Do not leave Jerusalem. Wait for what the Father has promised. . . . In a few days you will be baptized with the Holy Spirit" (Acts 1:4–5).

Jesus then led His disciples out to a place called Bethany, lifted His hands, and blessed them. At that moment, He went up into the sky and disappeared into a cloud. He went straight to heaven where "He sat down on the right side of God" (Mark 16:19). Then the disciples worshipped Jesus and went back to Jerusalem, full of joy.

. . . .

Learn More: Luke 24:50–53

The Holy Spirit Comes Down

*They were all filled with the Holy Spirit. Then they
began to speak in other languages which the
Holy Spirit made them able to speak.*
ACTS 2:4

EVENTS

It was the Feast of Pentecost, and 120 disciples were crowded into the large house of a wealthy disciple. Suddenly the sound of a mighty rushing wind filled the place where they were sitting.

What looked like tongues of fire came from heaven down to each of them. The Holy Spirit filled them inside, and they all began to praise God in other languages.

Jews had come from foreign lands to attend the feast. As the disciples rushed out of the house praising God, people were surprised that they were speaking the same languages that those from foreign lands spoke. Peter explained that this miracle fulfilled a prophecy of Joel in the Old Testament (Joel 2:28–32). Peter told the people that it was time for them to call on the name of the Lord to be saved. About 3,000 people made the decision to follow Jesus.

Learn More: Acts 2:1–21

Peter Raises Tabitha

Peter made them all leave the room. Then he got down on his knees and prayed. He turned to her body and said, "Tabitha, get up!" She opened her eyes and looked at Peter and sat up.
ACTS 9:40

Peter traveled around, preaching the Gospel. In the town of Joppa was a disciple named Tabitha, who made clothing for other believers and helped the poor. She became sick and died. Two men asked Peter to come to her home.

When Peter arrived, he was taken to the upper room where her body was. All the widows stood around, weeping and showing him the clothing that Tabitha had sewed.

Peter sent them all out of the room and then knelt and prayed. When he finished praying, he looked at her body; he said, "Tabitha, get up!" (Acts 9:40). Tabitha opened her eyes and sat up. Peter then called the disciples back into the room. News of this great miracle went all throughout Joppa, and many people believed in Jesus.

Learn More: Acts 9:36–43

EVENTS

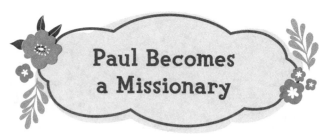

Paul Becomes a Missionary

All at once the earth started to shake. The stones under the prison shook and the doors opened. The chains fell off from everyone.
ACTS 16:26

Saul, for many years an enemy of Jesus, had gotten saved. Now known as Paul, he traveled around sharing the good news of the Gospel.

In the city of Athens, Greece, Paul was struck by how many idols and pagan temples there were. Towering over Athens was the Acropolis, filled with temples to the Greek gods.

Paul was preaching in the marketplace when some really smart people heard him. He taught how Jesus had risen from the dead, a strange idea to Greeks. So they brought him to Mars Hill to the city's ruling religious leaders.

Paul said he had seen an altar in their city with a message chiseled on the side: TO THE UNKNOWN GOD. Then he said, "You are worshiping Him without knowing Him. He is the One I will tell you about" (Acts 17:23). That "One" was Jesus!

Learn More: Acts 17:16–34

Jesus Returns to Earth

See! He is coming in the clouds. Every eye will see Him. Even the men who killed Him will see Him. All the people on the earth will cry out in sorrow because of Him. Yes, let it be so.
REVELATION 1:7

Why would someone like Paul give his life to tell people about Jesus? Because Jesus is coming back! He will come on the clouds of heaven with power and glory. Then the angels "will gather God's people together from the four winds" (Matthew 24:31).

When he was on an island called Patmos, Jesus' disciple and friend John the apostle had a vision. Jesus was sitting on a cloud, holding a harvesting tool. He then "harvested" the earth, taking all those who believe in Him with Him to heaven (Revelation 14:14–16) .

When we choose to follow Jesus, we can face even the hardest times on earth with hope. We know that He will someday take us to heaven to be with Him.

Learn More: Matthew 24:3–31

Heaven Comes to Earth

Then I saw a new heaven and a new earth.
The first heaven and the first earth had
passed away. There was no more sea.
REVELATION 21:1

At the end of time, God will make the earth new and create new heavens. There will be "no more sea." This probably means that there will be plenty of land for people to live on.

Then the city of light, "New Jerusalem," will come down out of the heavens and settle on earth. God Himself lives in that city, so He will then be living on this beautiful new planet with all those who believe in Him. This will be the beautiful ending to the long history of God's dealings with people. And it will be the beginning of His wonderful eternity!

Learn More: Revelation 21

Baptism

*When you were baptized, you were buried as Christ
was buried. When you were raised up in baptism,
you were raised as Christ was raised. You were
raised to a new life by putting your trust in God.
It was God Who raised Jesus from the dead.*
COLOSSIANS 2:12

Baptism shows that a person believes in God and has put their faith in Jesus. It was first seen in the ministry of John the Baptist. He told people to repent and be baptized to show their sin was washed away. Jesus asked John to baptize Him at the beginning of His ministry. By doing that, He showed an example for all people who would believe and be baptized in His name.

Christian groups continue to baptize believers of Christ. There are different ways baptism is done, whether by dunking in water or sprinkling. But the purpose of baptism is to remember the death, burial, and resurrection of Jesus Christ. It is a celebration of the new life Jesus gives to those who accept Him as Lord and Savior.

IDEAS

Learn More: Romans 6:4

Blessing

*When someone does something bad to you, do not
do the same thing to him. When someone talks about
you, do not talk about him. Instead, pray that good
will come to him. You were called to do this so
you might receive good things from God.*
1 Peter 3:9

A blessing is a kindness spoken or shown to another person. God blesses people, and people can also bless each other (Genesis 49:1–28).

In the Old Testament, a blessing carried great power. Once a blessing was spoken, it could not be changed or given to someone else (Genesis 27:30–35). Jacob tricked his father, Isaac, into blessing him instead of his older brother, so Esau did not receive the blessing that was meant for him.

God is the Giver of all blessings, and He wants to bless all people. Since His Son, Jesus, came into the world, His greatest blessing is to those who believe in Christ as their Savior. God blesses His people by forgiving our sins and giving us eternal life.

Learn More: Genesis 12:2

Born Again

Jesus said to him, "For sure, I tell you, unless a man is born again, he cannot see the holy nation of God."
JOHN 3:3

Being "born again" means becoming a member of God's family—becoming His child. The phrase comes from Jesus' talk with Nicodemus, a religious leader who went to Jesus to ask questions to learn more about Him.

Nicodemus didn't understand the idea. He wondered how a person could be born from his mom a second time. Jesus explained that He was talking about a new birth inside—in a person's spirit.

The apostle Paul described being born again in his letter to Christians in Corinth. "If a man belongs to Christ, he is a new person. The old life is gone. New life has begun" (2 Corinthians 5:17).

When people give Jesus control of their lives, instead of themselves, their sins are forgiven, and the Holy Spirit comes to live inside of them.

IDEAS

Learn More: John 3:1–17

Church

*"And I tell you that you are Peter. On this rock
I will build My church. The powers of hell will
not be able to have power over My church."*
MATTHEW 16:18

. . . .

A church is a group of people who believe in Jesus and gather together for worship (Acts 15:4). "The church" is all those who have ever lived who chose to allow Christ to be their Savior (Ephesians 5:27). The church is supposed to continue the work of Jesus in the world.

It began with the coming of the Holy Spirit on Jesus' followers on the day of Pentecost (Acts 2:1–6).

Toward the end of His life on earth, Jesus told His followers to spread the good news about His life, death, and resurrection throughout the world (Matthew 28:18–20). The book of Acts tells how the Holy Spirit gave the early church power to carry out this command.

. . . .

Learn More: Colossians 1:18

Communion

When we give thanks for the fruit of the vine at the Lord's supper, are we not sharing in the blood of Christ? The bread we eat at the Lord's supper, are we not sharing in the body of Christ?
1 CORINTHIANS 10:16

On the night before He was arrested and crucified, Jesus ate the Lord's Supper with His disciples. They came to Jesus in Jerusalem to eat a meal together in celebration of the Jewish Passover. Jesus used the things they ate and drank to tell about His coming death on the cross.

He said that the bread and wine they ate and drank together were a reminder of His body that would bleed to save people from sin. He also told them to remember His death whenever they ate this meal in the future.

The Lord's Supper is still celebrated by churches. Some other names it is known by are Holy Communion, the Eucharist, and the Lord's Table.

IDEAS

Learn More: Luke 22:19–20

Confession

It will not go well for the man who hides his sins, but he who tells his sins and turns from them will be given loving-pity.
PROVERBS 28:13

The word *confess* appears many times in the Bible. It means to admit or take responsibility for your sin and to turn to God for forgiveness.

Another kind of confession is telling others about your faith in Jesus. The apostle Paul said it is important to *confess* to others that you are a Christ follower, telling them that Jesus is Lord of your life. Paul wrote, "If you say with your mouth that Jesus is Lord, and believe in your heart that God raised Him from the dead, you will be saved from the punishment of sin. When we believe in our hearts, we are made right with God. We tell with our mouth how we were saved from the punishment of sin" (Romans 10:9–10).

Learn More: James 5:16

Courage

"Be strong and have strength of heart. For you will bring the people in to take this land which I promised to their fathers to give them."

JOSHUA 1:6

God spoke these words to Joshua when he became the leader of the Israelites after Moses died. God promised Joshua that He would be with him, just as He had done with Moses. Joshua had courage and led the Israelites to conquer the Canaanites and make the land their home.

Another example of courage is the prophet Jeremiah. For years, he warned the people of Judah they would be overtaken by a foreign nation unless they followed God. He was made fun of and put in prison. But God always showed His love to Jeremiah and protected him.

Some people think courage is not being afraid when there is danger. But a better way to think of courage is that it is knowing how to control fear. Scary things will happen, but God gives strength to have peace instead of fear.

Learn More: Deuteronomy 31:6

Creation

*"Our Lord and our God, it is right for You to have
the shining-greatness and the honor and the power.
You made all things. They were made and have
life because You wanted it that way."*
REVELATION 4:11

The Bible tells us that God existed before the world began. It was God who created the universe from nothing, simply by speaking. We learn about creation in Genesis 1, which gives details of everything God created in six days. On the sixth day, He made humans and gave them the responsibility of taking care of all of the plants and animals He made in the days before.

God has kept the world and everything in it running in an orderly way. The prophet Jeremiah said, "When He speaks, there is a storm of waters in the heavens. He makes the clouds rise from the ends of the earth. He makes lightning for the rain, and brings out the wind from His store-houses" (Jeremiah 10:13).

Learn More: Genesis 1

Crucifixion

*Then Pilate handed Him over to be nailed to
a cross. They took Jesus and led Him away.*
JOHN 19:16

Crucifixion was a form of punishment that the Roman government used for killing the worst criminals. A person's wrists were nailed to a beam of wood, which was attached to a stake in the ground. Sometimes the person's feet were nailed to the stake. As the person hung on the cross, breathing became very difficult. It was a slow, painful way to die.

In Jesus' time, crucifixion was a dishonorable way to die. But by His sacrifice, Jesus turned the cross into a badge of honor (Philippians 2:5–8).

Learn More: John 19:17–37

IDEAS

Eternity

But You and Your name, O Lord, will always be forever and to all people for all time.
PSALM 102:12

. . . .

People are limited by time—we are born on a certain date and we die on another date. This is not true of God. Not only has God existed forever—since before time began—but He will exist for all time to come. He is the eternal One who has no beginning or end.

It's difficult for people to understand eternity because we think of everything in terms of time. To us, a lifetime of 70 or 80 years seems long, but this is no more than the blink of an eye from God's perspective.

The God who lives forever shares the blessing of eternity with those who believe in His Son. "God's free gift is life that lasts forever. It is given to us by our Lord Jesus Christ" (Romans 6:23).

. . . .

Learn More: 2 Corinthians 4:18

Evil

The eyes of the Lord are in every place,
watching the bad and the good.
PROVERBS 15:3

Sin and evil entered the world when Adam and Eve disobeyed God's command in the Garden of Eden, eating the fruit God had told them to avoid (Genesis 3:6). The sin that began back then is the cause of the evil and suffering in our world today.

God gave the first humans freedom to make their own choices, and He gives us that same freedom. We can choose to love God and follow Him. Or we can choose to follow our sin and selfishness. But that will lead us to a life of trouble and destruction.

Thankfully, we have a loving Father who forgives us of our sinful choices because Jesus died on the cross for those sins.

IDEAS

Learn More: Romans 7:7–25

Faith

Now faith is being sure we will get what we hope for. It is being sure of what we cannot see.
HEBREWS 11:1

Hebrews 11 is known as the "faith chapter" of the New Testament. The writer begins the chapter with a definition of faith—trust in God, whom we cannot see but who is living and can work in our lives.

Salvation is only possible because of God's grace. But it is not complete without faith—that is, accepting Jesus Christ as Savior and Lord. As the apostle Paul said, "By His loving-favor you have been saved from the punishment of sin through faith. It is not by anything you have done. It is a gift of God" (Ephesians 2:8).

Learn More: Romans 1:17

Forgiveness

You must be kind to each other. Think of the other person. Forgive other people just as God forgave you because of Christ's death on the cross.

EPHESIANS 4:32

. . . .

To be forgiven is to have someone excuse the wrong done against him or her. Forgiveness among people is possible because of God's forgiveness of our sin against Him.

Human sin deserves the Lord's punishment because it goes against His holiness. In Old Testament times, God accepted an animal sacrifice as a way for people to pay for their sins and receive His forgiveness. In the New Testament, when Jesus died on the cross, He became the sacrifice for the sins of people. He is the reason anyone can be forgiven by God! Because we have been forgiven through Jesus' sacrifice, we are expected to be generous in our forgiveness of others.

. . . .

Learn More: Matthew 18:21–22

IDEAS

Giving

Each man should give as he has decided in his heart.
He should not give, wishing he could keep it. Or he
should not give if he feels he has to give. God loves
a man who gives because he wants to give.
2 CORINTHIANS 9:7

This verse is part of the apostle Paul's request to the Christians of Corinth to give to an offering for needy believers in Jerusalem. He did not tell them the amount that each believer should give. He wanted the gifts to be whatever a person felt like they wanted to give. Paul wanted the people to give from the right heart—not with a frown on their face or because they were forced into it.

They were to give out of a spirit of love because God's love was shown to us through His Son, Jesus Christ. True love is always giving itself away.

Learn More: Matthew 25:31–46

IDEAS

Gospel

I am not ashamed of the Good News. It is the power of God. It is the way He saves men from the punishment of their sins if they put their trust in Him. It is for the Jew first and for all other people also.

ROMANS 1:16

. . . .

The word for *Gospel* in the New Testament means "good news." That's exactly what the Gospel is—the good news that we can be saved from our sins. Why? Because God the Father has offered salvation through His Son, Jesus Christ.

Jesus is more than someone who tells the good news—He *is* the Good News. God's good news to all people was in Jesus' teachings, but it was also in His death and His resurrection.

The good news of the Gospel continues to be powerful in the world today through the work of the Holy Spirit in the church. All believers are called to share this good news with other people.

. . . .

Learn More: Matthew 4:23

Grace

*Then our Lord gave me much of His loving-favor and
faith and love which are found in Christ Jesus.*
1 TIMOTHY 1:14

. . . .

Grace is God's favor given to sinful human beings who
don't deserve it. The biggest expression of God's grace
was the gift of His Son, Jesus, to the world. Christ was
the perfect example of grace, bringing it to sinful people
so that they could be saved (Titus 2:11).

God's grace is one of the main points in the writings
of the apostle Paul. At first, he was unkind and punished
the people of the church. But Paul's heart was changed
by God's grace, and he became a bold missionary, sharing the Gospel with everyone around him. In all of his
writings, he made it clear he thanked God for His grace
and for how it can change a person's life.

. . . .

Learn More: 1 Corinthians 15:9–10

Healing

Jesus went over all Galilee. He taught in their places of worship and preached the Good News of the holy nation. He healed all kinds of sickness and disease among the people.
MATTHEW 4:23

Jesus came into the world to give humans a way to be saved from sin. But He was also concerned about those who suffered from physical problems. He healed many people during His earthly ministry.

Jesus also gave His disciples the power to heal people (Luke 9:2). They continued after Jesus went back to heaven. Peter and John the apostle healed a lame beggar at the temple in Jerusalem by calling on the name of Jesus and commanding him to "get up and walk" (Acts 3:6).

The book of James gives us a similar command, to lay hands on people and pray for their healing. The Holy Spirit gives us power too, just as Jesus and His disciples had power.

IDEAS

Learn More: James 5:13–18

153

Heaven

It is the same power that raised Christ from the dead.
This same power put Christ at God's right side in heaven.
EPHESIANS 1:20

Heaven is such a beautiful place that human words cannot describe it. But the words of the Bible writers paint a picture of what heaven is like.

Heaven is a place where we will enjoy fellowship with God for eternity (Revelation 21:3). While heaven itself will be beautiful, our greatest joy will come from being with the Lord.

In heaven, believers will be together again with their relatives and friends who had also chosen to follow Jesus. "Those of us who are still living here on earth will be gathered together with them in the clouds. We will meet the Lord in the sky and be with Him forever" (1 Thessalonians 4:17).

Learn More: Revelation 11:15–19

Holiness

For God has not called us to live in sin.
He has called us to live a holy life.
1 THESSALONIANS 4:7

. . . .

Holiness is one of the qualities of God's character. Throughout the Bible, He reminds His people, "Be holy, for I the Lord your God am holy" (Leviticus 19:2).

To be holy means to be "set apart." God's holiness set Him apart from humans or any other part of His creation. He cannot do anything impure, imperfect, or sinful.

Jesus was the perfect example of holiness. It's not possible in this life for weak and sinful human beings to have the level of holiness that belongs to the three persons of the Trinity—Father, Son, and Holy Spirit. But the Bible does say that believers should grow toward this way of life (1 Peter 1:15–16).

. . . .

Learn More: 1 Peter 2:5

IDEAS

Hope

Happy is he whose help is the God of Jacob,
and whose hope is in the Lord his God.
PSALM 146:5

Most people think of hope as a feeling that what they want to happen will happen. For believers in Jesus, hope is a strong faith in God's promises. Hope does not come from what we want but from God, who is our reason for hope.

The Bible warns about placing hope in things that are not going to last. These include wealth (Proverbs 11:28), military power (Isaiah 31:1–3), and earthly rulers (Psalm 146:3). Only the Lord should be our hope.

A Christian can put hope in Jesus because He died and rose again to save us. And with hope, we can look forward to His return and His promise of eternity with Him.

Learn More: Hebrews 6:19–20

IDEAS

Jealousy

The Jews were filled with jealousy when they saw so many people. They spoke against the things Paul said by saying he was wrong. They also spoke against God.
ACTS 13:45

The jealousy in Acts 13 took place in the city of Antioch during Paul's first missionary journey. Paul was preaching in the city synagogue. The large crowd included many Gentiles (non-Jews). This made the Jews so angry that they threw him out of the city.

God used this jealousy to make His Gospel known. Paul knew that many Jews had their beliefs from tradition, but Gentiles were eager to hear about Jesus. From then on, Paul preached mainly to non-Jewish people.

People are confused by the Bible wording that the Lord is a "jealous" God (Exodus 34:14). Since He is holy and perfect, how can a word like *jealous* describe Him? This is just another way of saying that He does not want us to put anything else in the place He should have in our hearts and minds.

IDEAS

Learn More: Romans 11:11

Joy

The angel said to them, "Do not be afraid. See! I bring
you good news of great joy which is for all people."
LUKE 2:10

Some people think of joy as feeling happy. But there's an important difference between joy and happiness. A person is happy when everything is going well. We can have joy even when things aren't going well in our lives. It won't change, because our joy comes from knowing Jesus and remembering all of His promises.

The apostle Paul included joy as one of the nine spiritual fruit in Galatians 5:22–23. Joy is possible for people who love Jesus even when they go through hard times (James 1:2–3). The writer of Psalms says it this way: "You will show me the way of life. Being with You is to be full of joy. In Your right hand there is happiness forever" (Psalm 16:11).

Learn More: Psalm 95:1

Kindness

*For sure, You will give me goodness and
loving-kindness all the days of my life. Then I
will live with You in Your house forever.*
PSALM 23:6

Acts of kindness are a way we can show the nature of God. God is always generous and kind toward His people. In the Old Testament, it takes two words—*love* and *kindness*—to tell about this characteristic of the Lord. A writer of psalms said it like this: "Your loving-kindness and Your truth will always keep me safe" (Psalm 40:11).

God the Father showed His perfect kindness when He sent the gift of Jesus to the world. Jesus showed kindness when He paid the penalty for sin by dying on the cross. He actually took our punishment on Himself. All we need to do is accept His salvation as a gift.

The apostle Paul listed kindness as one of the traits of people who follow Jesus (Colossians 3:12).

IDEAS

Learn More: Ephesians 4:32

159

Kingdom of God

He said, "The time has come. The holy nation
of God is near. Be sorry for your sins, turn from
them, and believe the Good News."
MARK 1:15

. . . .

With these words, Jesus was saying that God's rule of grace in the world had begun. The kingdom of God would be shown through Jesus' miracles, teaching, and death on the cross.

In His parables (teaching stories), Jesus described the kingdom of God. One story, about a man planting seeds, shows that the kingdom will grow in the hearts of some people, while it is rejected by others (Matthew 13:3–8).

The kingdom of God is a real thing, right now, for those who accept Jesus as Savior. But it will not be complete until Jesus returns to earth. Then He will create a new heaven and new earth where Christians will have an eternal relationship with Him.

. . . .

Learn More: Romans 14:17

Love, Brotherly

*"I give you a new Law. You are to love each other.
You must love each other as I have loved you."*
JOHN 13:34

These words of Jesus to His disciples are a perfect example of brotherly love, or love for others. Jesus knew their love for one another would have to be strong to help them through the days before and after His death, resurrection, and return to heaven.

During His time on earth, Jesus said that the second greatest commandment in the law was to love your neighbor as yourself. He gave the Golden Rule as a guide for treating others well. He even told His disciples that they should not hate their enemies but love them instead.

In 1 Corinthians 13, the apostle Paul's "love chapter," true love is described as unselfish and wanting the best for others.

Learn More: James 2:8

Love, God's

But God showed His love to us. While we were still sinners, Christ died for us.

ROMANS 5:8

. . . .

God showed His love when He saved His people, the Israelites, from slavery, sent them food and water in the wilderness, and gave them a land of their own. Moses reminded the people of God's love when they were getting ready to go into the Promised Land (Deuteronomy 7:7–8).

God's love was shown to all people through Jesus. The greatest way God's love was shown was through Jesus' death on the cross for us. John the apostle wrote, "This is love! It is not that we loved God but that He loved us. For God sent His Son to pay for our sins with His own blood" (1 John 4:10).

. . . .

Learn More: John 3:16

IDEAS

Miracle

"How great are the special things He shows us! How powerful are His wonderful works!"
DANIEL 4:3

A miracle is something that happens that can't be explained by humans. It can only happen because of God and His power.

When Jesus was on earth, He did many miracles. They showed God's power and His love for people. "The blind are made to see. Those who could not walk are walking. Those who have had bad skin diseases are healed. Those who could not hear are hearing. The dead are raised up to life and the Good News is preached to poor people" (Matthew 11:5).

Miracles didn't stop when Jesus went back to heaven. His last words on earth were that those who love Him should keep healing and preaching the Gospel for His glory.

Learn More: Mark 16:15–20

IDEAS

Obedience

Samuel said, "Is the Lord pleased as much with burnt gifts as He is when He is obeyed? See, it is better to obey than to give gifts."
1 SAMUEL 15:22

King Saul disobeyed God's command to destroy all of the Amalekites' possessions he'd won in battle. When the prophet Samuel asked Saul about it, the king lied. Saul said he planned to offer the animals he'd kept as sacrifices to God. But Samuel told Saul that obedience to God's Word is better than giving a sacrifice to Him.

Obedience is a lot like listening. To hear God's commands is important, but to listen and *do* what He commands is real obedience.

In the New Testament, the apostle Paul wrote about the difference between the obedience of Jesus and the disobedience of Adam. Adam's disobedience brought sin and death into the world. But Jesus' obedience brought God's grace and righteousness to believers (Romans 5:19).

Learn More: 1 Peter 1:13–14

Offering

Give to the Lord the honor of His name.
Bring a gift and come into His holy place.
PSALM 96:8

An offering brought to the Lord in Old Testament times was placed on the altar by priests. These offerings were certain kinds of animals, wine, grain, or sometimes a complete meal. The sacrifices would cover the people's sins and restore fellowship with God.

When Jesus died on the cross for our sins, the Old Testament way of sacrificing was not needed anymore. The author of the book of Hebrews wrote that Jesus is able to save all people who ask Him to, without a need for an altar offering.

Now the offering that Christians give to God is obedience to His commands.

Learn More: Hebrews 10:5–10

IDEAS

Patience

I did not give up waiting for the Lord.
And He turned to me and heard my cry.
PSALM 40:1

Most people think of patience as waiting for something to get better. But in the Bible, God showed that forgiveness was a part of patience. He was patient with His people, the Israelites, when they turned away from Him and didn't do what He asked them to.

The apostle Peter talked about the Lord's patience, using the word *waiting*. He was saying that the Lord is "waiting" for people to turn to Him, because He "does not want any person to be punished forever. He wants all people to be sorry for their sins and turn from them" (2 Peter 3:9).

Learn More: James 5:7

IDEAS

Peace

The peace of God is much greater than the human mind can understand. This peace will keep your hearts and minds through Christ Jesus.
PHILIPPIANS 4:7

After Jesus rose from the dead, Jesus said to His disciples, "May you have peace" (John 20:19). These words were a common greeting used by Jewish people at that time.

When the disciples heard this greeting from Jesus, they may have remembered the promise He had already made to them: "Peace I leave with you. My peace I give to you. I do not give peace to you as the world gives. Do not let your hearts be troubled or afraid" (John 14:27). This let them know that Jesus would be with them through the Holy Spirit, even though He would no longer be there in person.

Since we have been given God's peace, we should live peacefully with all people.

Learn More: Ephesians 2:14

IDEAS

Perseverance

So then, Christian brothers, because of all this, be strong. Do not allow anyone to change your mind. Always do your work well for the Lord. You know that whatever you do for Him will not be wasted.
1 CORINTHIANS 15:58

IDEAS

Perseverance is staying strong, even when things get hard. This is what the apostle Paul wanted for the believers who lived in the city of Corinth. He wanted them to keep following Jesus so they would be witnesses for Him in a city that was famous for its people's bad behavior.

We are only saved because of our faith in Jesus. But perseverance in doing good things shows other people that we have faith. The book of James says, "Faith is dead when nothing is done" (James 2:26).

An example of perseverance is Jesus Himself. The author of Hebrews encouraged his readers to finish the "race" of a Christian life by following Jesus' example.

Learn More: Hebrews 12:1–15

Prayer

*We are sure that if we ask anything that
He wants us to have, He will hear us.*
1 John 5:14

In this verse, John the apostle says that the Lord has promised to hear us when we pray. The apostle Peter wrote, "The Lord watches over those who are right with Him. He hears their prayers" (1 Peter 3:12).

Most of us think of prayer as a time when we ask God for something. When we request Him to do something for ourselves or others, that is a prayer of "petition." But there is so much more to prayer. In our prayers, we should give our worship to God because He deserves our praise. Giving thanks is also an important part of prayer. And we can't forget to confess our sins and ask for His forgiveness as we pray.

Learn More: Philippians 4:6

IDEAS

Repentance

"I even preached to the people who are not Jews that they should be sorry for their sins and turn from them to God. I told them they should do things to show they are sorry for their sins."
ACTS 26:20

The apostle Paul wrote that repentance is the first part of salvation. Repentance includes telling God you have sinned and that you're sorry for it. You ask God to forgive you, and you choose not to do that sin anymore.

King David repented when he prayed to the Lord, "Wash me inside and out from my wrong-doing and make me clean from my sin" (Psalm 51:2).

In the New Testament, John the Baptist preached that people needed to repent and turn to the Lord (Matthew 3:2). Jesus told the people, "Be sorry for your sins, turn from them, and believe the Good News" (Mark 1:15).

Being sorry for sins is not just something to do when you begin to follow Jesus. Throughout your Christian life, when you sin, tell God you're sorry, ask His forgiveness, and decide not to do that sin again.

Learn More: Luke 15:7

IDEAS

Resurrection

If the dead are not raised, then Christ was not raised from the dead. If Christ was not raised from the dead, then what we preach to you is worth nothing. Your faith in Christ is worth nothing.
1 CORINTHIANS 15:13–14

The apostle Paul wrote about how important Jesus' resurrection was. His victory over death means that those who believe in Him will be given new life after they die.

One time, when Jesus talked with Martha, He said that He was "the resurrection and the life." That was a way of saying Jesus is the Master over life and death. Then He brought Martha's brother Lazarus back from death.

After He rose from the dead Himself, Jesus spent 40 days with His followers before He went back to heaven. During that time, they could see for themselves that He was alive. Then they told others what they knew to be true.

God the Father has blessed all Christian believers with hope "because Jesus was raised from the dead" (1 Peter 1:3).

IDEAS

Learn More: John 11:25

Salvation

"There is no way to be saved from the punishment of sin through anyone else. For there is no other name under heaven given to men by which we can be saved."
ACTS 4:12

The apostle Peter spoke the words of Acts 4:12 to the Jewish religious leaders in Jerusalem. They questioned him and John the apostle about healing a man who was not able to walk. Peter explained to them that he could only do the miracle because of Jesus, who had risen from the dead.

Faith in Jesus is the only way to be free from sin. Salvation is knowing and believing that you are a sinner and that Jesus died to bring you new life. This new life is one that makes a relationship with a perfect God possible.

Jesus came to earth to bring salvation to a world of people who were lost and had no hope. This salvation is offered to all people. Jesus' death on the cross can cover all sin. But a person must choose to believe in Jesus and follow Him to receive the gift of salvation.

Learn More: 1 Peter 1:8–9

Scripture

These Jews were more willing to understand than those in the city of Thessalonica. They were very glad to hear the Word of God, and they looked into the Holy Writings to see if those things were true.

ACTS 17:11

The people of Berea read through the Old Testament scriptures, wanting to make sure that what Paul said about Jesus being the Messiah was true. They wanted to learn more about God's written Word.

"All the Holy Writings," Paul once said, "are God-given and are made alive by Him" (2 Timothy 3:16). Because the Bible is from God, it tells us how to live the way He wants us to.

The scriptures are full of wisdom to help us make good choices. They can help us feel better in sad times. They give us the knowledge we need to do what is right. And they show us how to want the praise of God more than the praise of people in everything we do.

Learn More: Romans 15:4

IDEAS

Sin

If we live in the light as He is in the light, we share what we have in God with each other. And the blood of Jesus Christ, His Son, makes our lives clean from all sin.

1 JOHN 1:7

. . . .

Sin came into the world when Adam and Eve disobeyed God in the Garden of Eden—and sin has been a part of the human race ever since. King David declared, "There is no one who does good" (Psalm 14:1).

When we disobey God and sin, we can't have everything God wants for our lives. But sin is not only doing what is wrong. We also sin when we don't do what we know is right. Jesus died for any sin we could ever do, but that doesn't ever make it okay to sin.

The punishment of sin is death. But God's generous gift is forgiveness for all of our sins and eternal life because Jesus died for us (Romans 6:23).

. . . .

Learn More: James 4:17

IDEAS

Spiritual Fruit

But the fruit that comes from having the Holy Spirit in our lives is: love, joy, peace, not giving up, being kind, being good, having faith, being gentle, and being the boss over our own desires. The Law is not against these things.
GALATIANS 5:22–23

In Galatians, there are nine words that describe the life of a person who follows Jesus. They show that Christians allow their lives to be controlled by the Holy Spirit. These nine qualities are known as the "fruit of the Spirit." Jesus said that other people will be able to see the power of God because of this "fruit"(Matthew 7:19–20).

The list begins with love, an attitude of unselfishness that puts others' needs before our own. Joy and peace in the Lord give believers strength in the good times and the bad times. Patience is the ability to keep being faithful to God. Kindness, gentleness, goodness, and self-control help us to show Jesus to all the people around us.

Learn More: James 3:17

Spiritual Gifts

But from your heart you should want the best gifts. Now I will show you even a better way.
1 CORINTHIANS 12:31

Spiritual gifts are talents and abilities the Holy Spirit gives to people who love Jesus. They will make believers grow stronger in their faith and help other believers too.

The apostle Paul wrote about spiritual gifts in a letter to the Christians at Corinth. In the church, people were arguing about some gifts being better or more important than others. But Paul reminded them that all gifts are important. They should all be shared, no matter how small they may seem.

The gifts listed in the letter include teaching, faith, healing, doing miracles, prophecy, discernment, speaking in tongues, and interpreting tongues. They should all be used to help other Christians and show those who don't know Jesus how important it is to follow Him.

Learn More: 1 Corinthians 12

Tithing

*"Honor and thanks be to God Most High,
Who has given into your hand those who
fought against you." Then Abram gave
Melchizedek a tenth of all he had taken.*
GENESIS 14:20

. . . .

Abraham gave a priest named Melchizedek ten percent (a "tithe") of what he had earned in battle. Abraham knew Melchizedek was also a worshipper of the one true God.

From then on, the Israelites, God's chosen people, would give a tithe to God. The law given to Moses said that they were to give ten percent of their crops and livestock as a special offering to God.

The New Testament does not say that a certain amount of giving is required. But those who love Jesus should be generous in sharing their money and possessions for God's work. Giving should be cheerful, from a heart of love for Jesus. He was the perfect example of generosity and sacrifice.

IDEAS

. . . .

Learn More: Luke 11:42

Worship

Come, let us bow down in worship. Let us get down on our knees before the Lord Who made us.
PSALM 95:6

. . . .

The word *worship* comes from an old English word *worth-ship*. Worship is love and attention given to a person or thing. But only the God of the universe is truly worthy of worship.

Real worship has several parts to it. The first is adoration, or praise. We should come to God with joyful praise because He is so good and shows us mercy.

Another part of worship is thanksgiving. When we thank God for His goodness, we are saying that we know we need Him.

We also should think about God's holiness. We sin, but He never has. We have hurt Him when we've sinned against Him, but He forgives us when we ask Him to and loves us with His perfect love. He deserves all of our worship!

. . . .

Learn More: Psalm 99:5

Abba, Father

He said, "Father, You can do all things.
Take away what must happen to Me. Even so,
not what I want, but what You want."
MARK 14:36

Abba is the name Jesus used for God the Father when He prayed in the garden of Gethsemane. It is an Aramaic word meaning "Father," similar to "Papa" in the English language.

The Jewish people usually would not have used this type of word for God. They thought of Him as someone who demanded more respect than that.

But it made sense for Jesus to call the Father *Abba*. As God's Son, He knew the Father more closely than anyone has ever known Him. Jesus Himself said, "I know My Father as My Father knows Me" (John 10:15). Through His death on the cross, Jesus made it possible for us to know God as a loving, forgiving Father too.

Learn More: John 10:37–38

Almighty God

*When Abram was ninety-nine years old, the Lord
came to him and said, "I am God All-powerful.
Obey Me, and be without blame."*
GENESIS 17:1

God had already promised Abram (later called Abraham)
that He would make his descendants a great nation and
give them a land of their own (Genesis 12:1–3; 13:15–17).
But Abraham did not have any children, so he couldn't
understand how that promise would happen.

By calling Himself "the All-powerful" in this verse,
God was telling Abraham that He had the power to make
miracles happen.

God can bless His people. And He has the power to
make that blessing as big as He thinks best. The apostle
Paul said, "God is able to do much more than we ask or
think through His power working in us" (Ephesians 3:20).

Learn More: Revelation 15:3

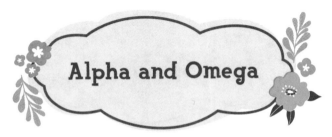

Alpha and Omega

*"I am the First and the Last.
I am the beginning and the end."*
REVELATION 22:13

. . . .

The name "Alpha and Omega" appears a few times in the Bible (see also Revelation 1:8, 11; 21:6). Alpha and omega were the first and last letters of the Greek alphabet—the language that most of the New Testament was written in. This name is a way of saying that Jesus is the beginning and the end of all things.

Jesus also said that He is "the First and the Last" (Revelation 1:17)—a name that means the same thing as Alpha and Omega. As the "First," He was with God the Father before the creation of the world (John 1:2). As the "Last," He will be there when the earth has its end (Revelation 22:10–12).

. . . .

Learn More: Revelation 2:8

NAMES OF GOD

Bread

Then Jesus said to the people, "For sure, I tell you, it was not Moses who gave you bread from heaven. My Father gives you the true Bread from heaven."
JOHN 6:32

In John 6, Jesus uses four different names for Himself, all using the word *bread*. He calls Himself "Bread from heaven" (verse 32), "Bread of God" (verse 33), "Bread of Life" (verse 35), and "Living Bread" (verse 51).

Bread was a big part of the history of Israel. The Lord kept His people alive in the wilderness after they escaped from Egypt by sending a special bread called manna for them to eat (Numbers 11:6–9).

Just as God sent food in the wilderness, He gives His people what they need for life today. As the Living Bread and the Bread of Life, Jesus gives the gift of eternal life to everyone who takes Him into their life.

Learn More: John 6:32–59

Chief Cornerstone

From now on you are not strangers and people who are not citizens. You are citizens together with those who belong to God. You belong in God's family. This family is built on the teachings of the missionaries and the early preachers. Jesus Christ Himself is the cornerstone, which is the most important part of the building.
EPHESIANS 2:19–20

A psalmist wrote, "The stone that was put aside by the workmen has become the most important stone in the building" (Psalm 118:22). This was a prophecy about the coming Messiah, Jesus.

Jesus knew that many Jews would not believe that He was the Messiah. He told the disciples that His gift of salvation would be offered to the Gentiles, other people who would accept Him as Lord and Savior (Matthew 21:42–43).

In the stone buildings of Bible times, a cornerstone was used to hold stones together at the point where they came together in a corner. Jesus is the Chief Cornerstone, the firm base of our faith. Although some may choose to reject Him, He is the hope of the world and the only way to eternal life.

Learn More: Isaiah 28:16

183

Christ

Simon Peter said, "You are the Christ,
the Son of the living God."
MATTHEW 16:16

The disciple Peter knew that Jesus was the "anointed One" who had been sent into the world by God Himself. Jesus was the Son of God, the Messiah, the One who would deliver the Jewish people.

Jesus praised Peter for knowing He was God's anointed. Jesus was really the Messiah—but the Jews were expecting a warrior, not a spiritual Savior. Even people who heard Him preach did not think He was the Messiah that Old Testament scripture had promised. But Jesus did not come to earth to be a political king. He came to teach about the kingdom of God, to heal the sick, and to save the people from their sin.

Learn More: Luke 9:20

Comforter

"Then I will ask My Father and He will give you another
Helper [Comforter]. He will be with you forever."
JOHN 14:16

Jesus said these words after He had told the disciples that He would die soon. He would not be with them as a human anymore, but He was not leaving them alone: He would send a "Comforter," the Holy Spirit, to be with them and give them the power to share the Gospel.

Jesus called the Holy Spirit "another" Comforter. The Greek word He used means "another of the same kind." Jesus Himself was the Comforter of His disciples, and He was sending another like Himself to be with them when He returned to heaven. The Holy Spirit would be so close that it would seem as if Jesus had never left.

Learn More: Acts 9:31

NAMES OF GOD

Creator

Have you not known? Have you not heard? The God Who lives forever is the Lord, the One Who made the ends of the earth. He will not become weak or tired. His understanding is too great for us to begin to know.
ISAIAH 40:28

. . . .

The prophet Isaiah could not believe that the people of Judah were turning away from the one true God. And they were worshipping false gods instead! The Creator God had made the universe by the power of His word. The idols had no power at all.

From the first chapter of the Bible, we learn important truths about God's creation. (1) He created our world from nothing. (2) He placed order and design into the universe. (3) Humans are the highest part of God's creation. (4) The Lord has given us the responsibility to take care of His world.

As Isaiah reminded the people of his nation, only our Creator God is worthy of our worship.

. . . .

Learn More: Genesis 1

Door

*"I am the Door. Anyone who goes in through
Me will be saved from the punishment of sin."*
JOHN 10:9

A door is an opening or entryway into a place. By saying that He was the Door, Jesus meant He was the only way to salvation and eternal life.

In His Sermon on the Mount, Jesus talked about two doors (Matthew 7:13–14). The wide door, meaning the way of the world, was easy to walk through. It stands for doing whatever you want to do in life. But the narrow door, which means following Jesus and His teachings, is tougher to enter. It takes sacrifice to follow Jesus.

But don't forget that He said, "I am the Way and the Truth and the Life. No one can go to the Father except by Me" (John 14:6).

Learn More: John 10:7–10

NAMES OF GOD

Everlasting Father

For to us a Child will be born. To us a Son will be given. And the rule of the nations will be on His shoulders. His name will be called Wonderful, Teacher, Powerful God, Father Who Lives Forever, Prince of Peace.

ISAIAH 9:6

- -

We usually talk about God as the Father and Jesus as the Son. But in this passage, Isaiah calls Jesus the "Father Who Lives Forever."

Jesus is one Person of the Trinity—God who is three Persons in One. This is very hard to understand, but we believe it by faith. Faith is believing in something we cannot completely know by ourselves. Because Jesus is God just as the Father is God, we know that Jesus was there before the beginning of the world. And He will not have any end. He lives forever, and He will love us forever!

- -

Learn More: Isaiah 40:28

Gift of God

The free gift of God is not like Adam's sin. God told Adam he was guilty because of his sin and through this one came sin and guilt. But the free gift makes men right with God. Through One, Christ, men's sins are forgiven.
ROMANS 5:16

. . . .

A gift is something a person gives to someone else without expecting anything in return. God gave us His Son, a gift we did not deserve and could never earn.

Most of us have received gifts that we couldn't use or that had to be returned because they were the wrong size or color. That is not so with God's gift of His Son, Jesus. It was a plan since the beginning of the world, it was given in love, and we needed this gift more than anything in the world.

"For God so loved the world that He gave His only Son. Whoever puts his trust in God's Son will not be lost but will have life that lasts forever" (John 3:16).

. . . .

Learn More: Matthew 7:11

God

Thomas said to Him, "My Lord and my God!"
JOHN 20:28

. . . .

When "Doubting Thomas" finally saw Jesus after He rose from the dead, it was proof that everything he had heard was true. He also understood that Jesus was the Son of God. The verse above is one of the clearest statements that Jesus *is* God. Thomas, like all the other disciples, had lived and worked with Jesus for three years. They had seen His miracles and heard His teachings. They knew that Jesus had power. But it took them longer to understand that Jesus was actually God in a human body.

Being God and man at the same time, Jesus is both all-powerful and able to understand the struggles that we as people face.

. . . .

Learn More: 1 Timothy 3:16

Good Shepherd

"I am the Good Shepherd. The Good Shepherd gives His life for the sheep."
JOHN 10:11

Sheep are helpless animals that can't defend themselves against other animals that could harm them, like wolves and lions. Jesus calls His followers sheep and Himself the Shepherd who leads His flock (John 10:1–16).

The shepherd needs to constantly watch the sheep. If he doesn't, the sheep could wander away and get hurt. They need to be led from one place to another to find food and water. They need a good leader, one who will protect them and provide for them.

Jesus is our Good Shepherd. He loves us (His sheep) and is the best leader we could ever have. He will always protect us and provide for us.

Learn More: Hebrews 13:20

NAMES OF GOD

Holy Spirit

Watch your talk! No bad words should be coming from your mouth. Say what is good. Your words should help others grow as Christians. Do not make God's Holy Spirit have sorrow for the way you live. The Holy Spirit has put a mark on you for the day you will be set free.
EPHESIANS 4:29–30

. . . .

God's Holy Spirit can be made sad by the sinful actions of Christians. This shows that the Holy Spirit is a person, not just some kind of invisible force. Only a person can experience emotions like sorrow, so the Spirit is a "He," not an "it." He is as much a person as God the Father and Jesus the Son.

If some actions by Christians make the Holy Spirit sad, it's also true that certain attitudes and behaviors bring Him pleasure. These include the spiritual fruit in the apostle Paul's famous list in Galatians 5:22–23.

. . . .

Learn More: John 14:26

I Am

Jesus said to them, "For sure, I tell you, before Abraham was born, I was and am and always will be!"
JOHN 8:58

. . . .

This name that Jesus called Himself, "I Am," is the same one God used for Himself when He spoke to Moses from the burning bush. Jesus was saying that He never had a beginning and He will never have an end—He had always been and He would always be.

This statement made the Jewish religious leaders angry, so they picked up stones to throw at Jesus. That was the penalty for anyone who said they were equal with God (Leviticus 24:16). But Jesus was able to get away from them before they hurt Him. He would not be arrested and crucified until it was the right moment in God's plan.

. . . .

Learn More: Exodus 3:14

NAMES OF GOD

Immanuel

A young woman, who has never had a man, will give birth to a son. She will give Him the name Immanuel.
ISAIAH 7:14

· ·

This prophecy from Isaiah was fulfilled with the birth of Jesus (Matthew 1:22–23). The name *Immanuel*, meaning "God with us," was given to Jesus even before He was born by an angel who appeared to Joseph. He had promised to marry a certain young woman but was concerned when he learned she was expecting a baby. We know her today as Mary, mother of Jesus.

From the earliest pages of the Old Testament, God had promised to be with His people. These promises reached their peak in God's Son, Jesus Christ. He came to earth in the form of a man to show that God is for us in our sinful and helpless condition. As man, He understands our temptations and failures. As God, He can meet all these needs through His love and grace.

· ·

Learn More: Hebrews 13:5

King of Kings

"These kings will fight and make war with the Lamb. But the Lamb will win the war because He is Lord of lords and King of kings. His people are the called and chosen and faithful ones."
REVELATION 17:14

. . . .

When Jesus comes back to earth, He will be wearing a banner with the phrase "King of Kings" on it. This name, telling of His power to rule over the whole earth, will be visible for everyone to see.

In Old Testament times, the title "king of kings" was given to a ruler with an area that covered a large territory. When Jesus returns, He will come as the Ruler of the whole universe. If we have asked Him to be our Lord, we are subjects in His kingdom. He is King over our lives and King over the church.

. . . .

Learn More: Revelation 19:16

NAMES OF GOD

Lamb of God

The next day John the Baptist saw Jesus coming to him. He said, "See! The Lamb of God Who takes away the sin of the world!"
JOHN 1:29

John the Baptist could have used any name for Jesus, but he chose "Lamb of God." Lambs were young sheep used as sacrificial animals in Jewish worship (Leviticus 14:11–13). At the very beginning of Jesus' ministry, John understood why Jesus came to earth and that He would be the sacrifice for all people.

On the night before He was crucified, Jesus and His disciples gathered to celebrate the meal together. It was a part of the Jewish festival of Passover. As Jesus passed the cup to the disciples, He said, "This is My blood of the New Way of Worship which is given for many. It is given so the sins of many can be forgiven" (Matthew 26:28).

Learn More: Hebrews 9:12

Light of the World

Jesus spoke to all the people, saying, "I am the Light of the world. Anyone who follows Me will not walk in darkness. He will have the Light of Life."
JOHN 8:12

. . . .

Jesus was sent by God the Father as a Savior for all people. This is one reason the religious leaders of that time didn't like Him. They didn't think it would be right for God to love the people of the world as much as He would love the Jewish leaders. They thought they knew all about how the Messiah would treat them when He came.

This problem is still here today. Some people think that Jesus would do certain things and wouldn't do other things. They believe they know exactly how He would act. But Jesus came for everyone—poor people, people with problems, and people who haven't heard of Him yet. He has come to be a Light for all, and His light will never get dim or go out.

. . . .

Learn More: John 9:5

NAMES OF GOD

Messiah

*The woman said to Him, "I know the Jews
are looking for One Who is coming. . . .
When He comes, He will tell us everything."*
JOHN 4:25

Jesus let the Samaritan woman at the well in on a secret—that He was the Messiah, the deliverer God had promised to send to His people for hundreds of years. She knew the "One Who is coming" would be able to explain what she couldn't understand. But He told her that He was the One she was waiting for.

The Jewish people expected their messiah to be a political and military deliverer who would conquer Rome and restore Israel. Jesus had come into the world as the spiritual Messiah. They knew to expect His arrival; they just didn't understand what His purpose would be.

Learn More: Daniel 9:25–26

Redeemer

"But as for me, I know that the One Who bought me and made me free from sin lives, and that He will stand upon the earth in the end."
JOB 19:25

The name *Redeemer* ("the One Who bought me") in Bible times described the nearest relative who would rescue a family member who was in trouble. So, if a person lost his property because of a debt, his *kinsman-redeemer* would buy it and give it back to the relative.

The prophet Isaiah wrote that God is the Redeemer who will come to the rescue of His people. What Isaiah and Job only hoped for has now happened. Any trouble we face will be taken care of by our Redeemer, the One who will rescue us. We can trust that Jesus will take care of us.

Learn More: Isaiah 59:20

Rock

"There is no one holy like the Lord. For sure, there is no one other than You. There is no rock like our God."
1 SAMUEL 2:2

Hannah prayed this prayer when she brought her son Samuel to Eli the priest. God had answered her prayer and gave her a son, and she kept her promise to give him back to the Lord. She knew that God would always keep His promises.

The word *rock* describing God appears often in the book of Psalms. King David praised God for being his Rock of defense against King Saul.

"Rock," when used of God, doesn't mean a small stone, but a mountainside. There are large rock formations that can be seen throughout the land of Israel. Mountains of solid rock can protect from natural dangers and enemies, just as God the Father protects us and keeps us safe.

Learn More: Psalm 94:22

Savior

"There is no other God besides Me, a God Who is right and good, a God Who saves. There is none except Me."
ISAIAH 45:21

A *savior* is a person who rescues someone from danger. This name is used for God in the Old Testament, and it often tells about God rescuing people from a bad situation. God sent plagues against the Egyptians when Pharaoh didn't allow the Israelites to leave his country. The plagues were God's way of saving His own people from slavery.

The New Testament talks less of people being saved from hard times and more of people being saved from their sins. Jesus came as Savior of the world. When He took our sins on Himself, He made it so that we can have a relationship with God.

Learn More: 1 Timothy 4:10

NAMES OF GOD

Strength

"The Lord is my strength and song. He is the One Who saves me. He is my God and I will praise Him. He is my father's God and I will honor Him."

EXODUS 15:2

. . . .

Moses and the Israelites sang Exodus 15:2 as a song of praise to the Lord. God had just saved them from the army of Egyptians who were chasing after them. The people had seen His power when He parted the waters of the Red Sea and allowed them all to walk safely through to the other side. It makes sense that Moses would call God his "strength."

Our God will always have enough strength to take care of His children anywhere, anytime. The prophet Isaiah said, "He gives strength to the weak. And He gives power to him who has little strength" (Isaiah 40:29).

. . . .

Learn More: Isaiah 40:28–31

NAMES OF GOD

Truth

Jesus said, "I am the Way and the Truth and the Life.
No one can go to the Father except by Me."
JOHN 14:6

Our world tells us that there are many different views of truth. Some people think they will find truth if they get a lot of money and possessions. Others think that getting knowledge leads to truth. Many people think that each person needs to find "their own truth," and that can be different for each one.

Jesus told Pilate that He had come into the world to "speak about the truth." But Pilate asked, "What is truth?" (John 18:37–38). The Truth—Jesus—was so close to Pilate that he could reach out and touch it, but he missed it because he didn't believe. As believers, we *know* the Truth. He will give us the help we need to learn what is right and what is wrong.

Learn More: John 8:32

Vine

"I am the Vine and you are the branches. Get your life from Me. Then I will live in you and you will give much fruit. You can do nothing without Me."
JOHN 15:5

- -

The vine that Jesus was talking about was a grapevine. It had one main stem with several smaller stems going off in all directions. These smaller branches needed to depend completely on the main stem.

Jesus told His disciples that they should depend completely on Him as their Lord and Savior. He as "the Vine" would provide for them so they would grow "much fruit." And being a branch, or showing this spiritual fruit to those around them, could make others want to be followers of Christ too.

- -

Learn More: Isaiah 5:1–2

Way

Jesus said, "I am the Way and the Truth and the Life. No one can go to the Father except by Me."

<small>JOHN 14:6</small>

. . . .

The disciple Thomas was confused by Jesus' statement that He would leave soon after He rose from the dead (John 14:1–4). Thomas wanted to know how he and the other disciples could find Jesus after He left. Thomas was reminded that Jesus was the only "way" to heaven.

Sometimes thinking about heaven can make us forget about Jesus Himself. We wonder where heaven will be and what it will look like. We will never know the answers to these questions until we get there. But we do know the most important thing: Jesus is the only way to that wonderful place.

. . . .

Learn More: John 14:1–7

NAMES OF GOD

Word

The Word (Christ) was in the beginning. The Word was with God. The Word was God.

John 1:1

The beginning of the Gospel of John teaches about Jesus as the eternal Son who was with God the Father before the world was created. Jesus was "in the beginning" (John 1:1) as the eternal Word and is the same God who was "in the beginning" (Genesis 1:1) creating the heavens and the earth.

Jesus is called "the Word" because He is where wisdom comes from, and He helps us to understand the Bible. Through His Word and His example from when He was on earth, we can learn about God and how we can live a life that honors Him.

Learn More: John 1:1–5

ANOTHER GREAT BOOK FOR GIRLS!

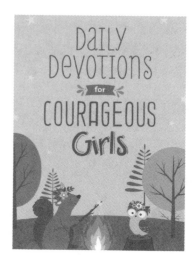

God's Word makes girls courageous. . .and you'll experience His unchanging truth firsthand in this daily devotional in the popular Courageous Girls series. With each turn of the page, you'll see how God is working—every day—to grow you into the faithful, courageous girl you were created to be.

Paperback / 978-1-64352-524-2 / $9.99